STANISLAW LEM

Solaris

Translated by Joanna Kilmartin and Steve Cox

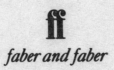

faber and faber

First published in 1970
by Faber and Faber Limited
3 Queen Square London WC1N 3AU
First published in this edition in 2003

Photoset by RefineCatch Limited, Bungay, Suffolk
Printed in England by Mackays of Chatham PLC

A CIP record for this book
is available from the British Library
ISBN 0–571–21972–1

2 4 6 8 10 9 7 5 3 1

Contents

The Arrival

At 19.00 hours, ship's time, I made my way to the launching bay. The men around the shaft stood aside to let me pass, and I climbed down into the capsule.

Inside the narrow cockpit, there was scarcely room to move. I attached the hose to the valve on my space suit and it inflated rapidly. From then on, I was incapable of making the smallest movement. There I stood, or rather hung suspended, enveloped in my pneumatic suit and yoke to the metal hull.

I looked up; through the transparent canopy I could see a smooth, polished wall and, far above, Moddard's head leaning over the top of the shaft. He vanished, and suddenly I was plunged in darkness: the heavy protective cone had been lowered into place. Eight times I heard the hum of the electric motors which turned the screws, followed by the hiss of the shock-absorbers. As my eyes grew accustomed to the dark, I could see the luminous circle of the solitary dial.

A voice echoed in my headphones:

'Ready, Kelvin?'

'Ready, Moddard,' I answered.

'Don't worry about a thing. The Station will pick you up in flight. Have a good trip!'

There was a grinding noise and the capsule swayed. My muscles tensed in spite of myself, but there was no further noise or movement.

'When is lift-off?' As I asked, I noticed a rustling outside, like a shower of fine sand.

'You're on your way, Kelvin. Good luck!' Moddard's voice sounded as close as before.

A wide slit opened at eye-level, and I could see the stars.

1

The *Prometheus* was orbiting in the region of Alpha in Aquarius and I tried in vain to orient myself; a glittering dust filled my porthole. I could not recognize a single constellation; in this region of the galaxy the sky was unfamiliar to me. I waited for the moment when I would pass near the first distinct star, but I was unable to isolate any one of them. Their brightness was fading; they receded, merging into a vague, purplish glimmer, the sole indication of the distance I had already travelled. My body rigid, sealed in its pneumatic envelope, I was knifing through space with the impression of standing still in the void, my only distraction the steadily mounting heat.

Suddenly, there was a shrill, grating sound, like a steel blade being drawn across a sheet of wet glass. This was it, the descent. If I had not seen the figures racing across the dial, I would not have noticed the change in direction. The stars having vanished long since, my gaze was swallowed up on the pale reddish glow of infinity. I could hear my heart thudding heavily. I could feel the coolness from the air-conditioning on my neck, although my face seemed to be on fire. I regretted not having caught a glimpse of the *Prometheus*, but the ship must have been out of sight by the time the automatic controls had raised the shutter of my porthole.

The capsule was shaken by a sudden jolt, then another. The whole vehicle began to vibrate. Filtered through the insulating layers of the outer skins, penetrating my pneumatic cocoon, the vibration reached me, and ran through my entire body. The image of the dial shivered and multiplied, and its phosphorescence spread out in all directions. I felt no fear. I had not undertaken this long voyage only to overshoot my target!

I called into the microphone:

'Station Solaris! Station Solaris! Station Solaris! I think I am leaving the flight-path, correct my course! Station Solaris, this is the *Prometheus* capsule. Over.'

I had missed the precious moment when the planet first

came into view. Now it was spread out before my eyes; flat, and already immense. Nevertheless, from the appearance of its surface, I judged that I was still at a great height above it, since I had passed that imperceptible frontier after which we measure the distance that separates us from a celestial body in terms of altitude. I was falling. Now I had the sensation of falling, even with my eyes closed. (I quickly reopened them: I did not want to miss anything there was to be seen.)

I waited a moment in silence before trying once more to make contact. No response. Successive bursts of static came through the headphones, against a background of deep, low-pitched murmuring, which seemed to me the very voice of the planet itself. A veil of mist covered the orange-coloured sky, obscuring the porthole. Instinctively, I hunched myself up as much as my inflated suit would allow, but almost at once I realized that I was passing through cloud. Then, as though sucked upwards, the cloud-mass lifted; I was gliding, half in light, half in shadow, the capsule revolving upon its own vertical axis. At last, through the porthole, the gigantic ball of the sun appeared, looming up on the left and disappearing to the right.

A distant voice reached me through the murmuring and crackling.

'Station Solaris calling! Station Solaris calling! The capsule will land at zero-hour. I repeat, the capsule will land at zero-hour. Stand by for count-down. Two hundred and fifty, two hundred and forty-nine, two hundred and forty-eight . . . '

The words were punctuated by sharp screeching sounds; automatic equipment was intoning the phrases of the reception-drill. This was surprising, to say the least. As a rule, men on space stations were eager to greet a newcomer, especially if he was arriving direct from Earth. I did not have long to ponder this, for the sun's orbit, which had so far encircled me, shifted unexpectedly, and the incandescent disc appeared now to the right, now to the left, seeming to dance on the planet's horizon. I was swinging like a giant pendulum while the planet, its surface wrinkled with purplish-blue and black furrows, rose up in front of me like a wall. As my head began to spin, I caught sight of a tiny pattern of green and white dots; it was the station's positioning-marker. Something detached itself with a snap from the cone of the capsule; with a fierce jerk, the long parachute collar released its hoops, and the noise which followed reminded me irresistibly of Earth: for the first time after so many months, the moaning of the wind.

Everything went quickly after this. So far, I had known that I must be falling; now I could see it for myself. The green and white chequer-board grew rapidly larger and I could see that it was painted on an elongated silvery body, shaped like a whale, its flanks bristling with radar antennae. This metal colossus, which was pierced with several rows of shadowy apertures, was not resting on the planet itself but suspended above it, casting upon the inky surface beneath an ellipsoidal shadow of even deeper blackness. I could make out the slate-coloured ripples of the ocean, stirring with a faint motion. Suddenly, the clouds rose to a great height, rimmed with a blinding crimson glare; the lurid sky became grey, distant and flat; everything was blotted out; I was falling in a spin.

A sharp jolt, and the capsule righted itself. Through the porthole, I could see the ocean once more, the waves like crests of glittering quicksilver. The hoops of the parachute, their cords snapped, flapped furiously over the waves, carried on the wind. The capsule gently descended, swaying with a peculiar slow-motion rhythm imposed on it by the artificial magnetic field; there was just time to glimpse the launching pads and the parabolic reflectors of two radio-telescopes on top of their pierced steel towers.

With the clang of steel rebounding against steel, the capsule came to a stop. A hatch opened, and with a long, harsh sigh, the metal shell which imprisoned me reached the end of its voyage.

I heard the mechanical voice from the control centre:

4

'Station Solaris. Zero and zero. The capsule has landed. Out.'

Feeling a vague pressure on my chest and a disagreeable heaviness in the pit of my stomach, I seized the control levers with both hands and cut the contacts. A green indicator lit up: 'ARRIVAL.' The capsule opened, and the pneumatic padding shoved me gently from behind, so that, in order to keep my balance, I had to take a step forward.

With a muffled sigh of resignation, the spacesuit expelled its air. I was free.

I found myself inside a vast, silver funnel, as high as a cathedral nave. A cluster of coloured pipes ran down the sloping walls and disappeared into rounded orifices. I turned round. The ventilation shafts were roaring, sucking in the poisonous gases from the planet's atmosphere which had infiltrated when my capsule had landed inside the Station. Empty, resembling a burst cocoon, the cigar-shaped capsule stood upright, enfolded by a calyx mounted on a steel base. The outer casing, scorched during flight, had turned a dirty brown.

I went down a small stairway. The metal floor below had been coated with a heavy-duty plastic. In places, the wheels of trolleys carrying rockets had worn through this plastic covering to expose the bare steel beneath.

The throbbing of the ventilators ceased abruptly and there was total silence. I looked around me, a little uncertain, waiting for someone to appear; but there was no sign of life. Only a neon arrow glowed, pointing towards a moving walkway which was silently unreeling. I allowed myself to be carried forward.

The ceiling of the hall descended in a fine parabolic arc until it reached the entrance to a gallery, in whose recesses gas cylinders, gauges, parachutes, crates and a quantity of other objects were scattered about in untidy heaps.

The moving walkway set me down at the far end of the

gallery, on the threshold of a dome. Here there was an even greater disorder. A pool of oily liquid spread out from beneath a pile of oil-drums; a nauseating smell hung in the air; footprints, in a series of glutinous smears, went off in all directions. The oil-drums were covered with a tangle of tick-ertape, torn paper and other waste.

Another green arrow directed me to the central door. Behind this stretched a narrow corridor, hardly wide enough for two men to walk side by side, lit by slabs of glass let into the ceiling. Then another door, painted in green and white squares, which was ajar; I went in.

The cabin had concave walls and a big panoramic window, which a glowing mist had tinged with purple. Outside the murky waves slid silently past. Open cupboards lined the walls, filled with instruments, books, dirty glasses, vacuum flasks – all covered with dust. Five or six small trolleys and some collapsible chairs cluttered up the stained floor. One chair alone was inflated, its back raised. In this armchair there was a little thin man, his face burnt by the sun, the skin on his nose and cheeks coming away in large flakes. I recognized him as Snow, a cybernetics expert and Gibarian's deputy. In his time he had published articles of great originality in the *Solarist Annual*. It so happened that I had never had the opportunity of meeting him. He was wearing a mesh shirt which allowed the grey hairs of his sunken chest to poke through here and there, and canvas trousers with a great many pockets, mechanic's trousers, which had once been white but now were stained at the knees and covered with holes from chemical burns. He was holding one of those pear-shaped plastic flasks which are used in spaceships not equipped with internal gravitational systems. Snow's eyes widened in amazement as he looked up and saw me. The flask dropped from his fingers and bounced several times, spilling a few drops of transparent liquid. Blood drained from his face. I was too astonished to speak, and this dumbshow continued for so long that Snow's terror gradually communicated itself to me. I took a step forward. He cringed in his chair.

'Snow?'

He quivered as though I had struck him. Gazing at me in indescribable horror, he gasped out:

'I don't know you . . .' His voice croaked. 'I don't know you . . . What do you want?'

The spilt liquid was quickly evaporating; I caught a whiff of alcohol. Had he been drinking? Was he drunk? What was he so terrified of? I stood in the middle of the room; my legs were trembling; my ears roared, as though they were stuffed with cotton-wool. I had the impression that the ground was giving way beneath my feet. Beyond the curved window, the ocean rose and fell with regularity. Snow's bloodshot eyes never left me. His terror seemed to have abated, but his expression of invincible disgust remained.

'What's the matter? Are you ill?' I whispered.

'You seem worried,' he said, his voice hollow. 'You actually seem worried . . . So it's like that now, is it? But why concern yourself about me? I don't know you.'

'Where's Gibarian?' I asked.

He gave a gasp and his glassy eyes lit up for an instant.

'Gi . . . Giba . . . No! No!'

His whole frame shook with stifled, hysterical laughter; then he seemed to calm down a little.

'So it's Gibarian you've come for, is it? Poor old Gibarian. What do you want with him?'

His words, or rather his tone of voice, expressed hatred and defiance; it was as though I had suddenly ceased to represent a threat to him.

Bewildered, I mumbled:

'What . . . Where is he?'

'Don't you know?'

Obviously he was drunk and raving. My anger rose. I should have controlled myself and left the room, but I had lost patience. I shouted:

7

'That's enough! How could I know where he is since I've only just arrived? Snow! What's going on here?'

His jaw dropped. Once again he caught his breath and his eyes gleamed with a different light. He seized the arms of his chair with both hands and stood up with difficulty. His knees were trembling.

'What? You've just arrived ... Where have you come from?' he asked, almost sober.

'From Earth!' I retorted angrily. 'Maybe you've heard of it? Not that anyone would ever guess it.'

'From Earth? Good God! Then you must be Kelvin.'

'Of course. Why are you looking at me like that? What's so startling about me?'

He blinked rapidly.

'Nothing,' he said, wiping his forehead, 'nothing. Forgive me, Kelvin, it's nothing, I assure you. I was simply surprised, I didn't expect to see you.'

'What do you mean, you didn't expect to see me? You were notified months ago, and Moddard radioed only today from the *Prometheus.*'

'Yes; yes, indeed. Only, you see, we're a bit disorganized at the moment.'

'So I see,' I answered dryly.

Snow walked around me, inspecting my atmosphere suit, which was standard issue with the usual harness of wires and cables attached to the chest. He coughed, and rubbed his bony nose:

'Perhaps you would like a bath? It would do you good. It's the blue door, on the other side.'

'Thanks – I know the Station layout.'

'You must be hungry.'

'No. Where's Gibarian?'

Without answering, he went over to the window. From behind he looked considerably older. His close-cropped hair was grey, and deep wrinkles creased his sunburnt neck.

The wave-crests glinted through the window, the colossal

8

rollers rising and falling in slow-motion. Watching the ocean like this one had the illusion – it was surely an illusion – that the Station was moving imperceptibly, as though teetering on an invisible base; then it would seem to recover its equilibrium, only to lean the opposite way with the same lazy movement. Thick foam, the colour of blood, gathered in the troughs of the waves. For a fraction of a second, my throat tightened and I thought longingly of the *Prometheus* and its strict discipline; the memory of an existence which suddenly seemed a happy one, now gone for ever.

Snow turned round, nervously rubbing his hands together.

'Listen,' he said abruptly, 'except for me there's no one around for the moment. You'll have to make do with my company for today. Call me Ratface; don't argue. You know me by my photograph, just imagine we're old friends. Everyone calls me Ratface, there's nothing I can do about it.'

Obstinately, I repeated my question:

'Where is Gibarian?'

He blinked again.

'I'm sorry to have received you like that. It's . . . it's not exactly my fault. I had completely forgotten . . . A lot has been happening here, you see . . .'

'It's all right. But what about Gibarian? Isn't he on the Station? Is he on an observation flight?'

Snow was gazing at a tangled mass of cables.

'No, he hasn't left the Station. And he won't be flying. The fact is . . .'

My ears were still blocked, and I was finding it more and more difficult to hear.

'What? What do you mean? Where is he then?'

'I should think you might guess,' he answered in a changed voice, looking me coldly in the eyes. I shivered. He was drunk, but he knew what he was saying.

'There's been an accident?'

He nodded vigorously, watching my reactions closely.

'When?'

'This morning, at dawn.'

By now, my sensations were less violent; this succinct exchange of questions and answers had calmed me. I was beginning to understand Snow's strange behaviour.

'What kind of accident?'

'Why not go to your cabin and take off your spacesuit? Come back in, say, an hour's time.'

I hesitated.

'All right,' I said finally.

As I made to leave, he called me back.

'Wait!' He had an uneasy look, as if he wanted to add something but was finding it difficult to bring out the words. After a pause, he said:

'There used to be three of us here. Now, with you, there are three of us again. Do you know Sartorius?'

'In the same way as I knew you – only from his photographs.'

'He's up there, in the laboratory, and I doubt if he'll come down before dark, but . . . In any case, you'll recognize him. If you should see anyone else – someone who isn't me or Sartorius, you understand, then . . .'

'Then what?'

I must be dreaming. All this could only be a dream! The inky waves, their crimson gleams under the low-hanging sun, and this little man who had gone back to his armchair, sitting there as before, hanging his head and staring at the heap of cables.

'In that case, do nothing.'

'Who could I see?' I flared up. 'A ghost?'

'You think I'm mad, of course. No, no, I'm not mad. I can't say anything more for the moment. Perhaps . . . who knows? . . . Nothing will happen. But don't forget I warned you.'

'Don't be so mysterious. What's all this about?'

10

'Keep a hold on yourself. Be prepared to meet . . . anything. It sounds impossible I know, but try. It's the only advice I can give you. I can't think of anything better.'

'But what could I possibly meet?' I shouted.

Seeing him sitting there, looking sideways at me, his sunburnt face drooping with fatigue, I found it difficult to contain myself. I wanted to grab him by the shoulders and shake him.

Painfully, dragging the words out one by one, he answered:

'I don't know. In a way, it depends on you.'

'Hallucinations, you mean?'

'No . . . it's real enough. Don't attack. Whatever you do, remember that!'

'What are you getting at?' I could hardly recognize the sound of my own voice.

'We're not on Earth, you know.'

'A Polytherian form?' I shouted. 'There's nothing human about them!'

I was about to rush at him, to drag him out of the trance, prompted, apparently, by his crazy theories, when he murmured:

'That's why they're so dangerous. Remember what I've told you, and be on your guard!'

'What happened to Gibarian?'

He did not answer.

'What is Sartorius doing?'

'Come back in an hour.'

I turned and went out. As I closed the door behind me, I took a last look at him. Tiny, shrunken, his head in his hands and his elbows resting on his stained knees, he sat there, motionless. It was only then that I noticed the dried bloodstains on the backs of his hands.

The Solarists

In the empty corridor I stood for a moment in front of the closed door. I noticed a strip of plaster carelessly stuck on one of the panels. Pencilled on it was the word 'Man!' At the sight of this faintly scribbled word, I had a sudden longing to return to Snow for company; but I thought better of it.

His crazy warnings still ringing in my ears, I started off down the narrow, tubular passage which was filled with the moaning of the wind, my shoulders bowed under the weight of the spacesuit. On tip-toe, half-consciously fleeing from some invisible watcher, I found two doors on my left and two more on my right. I read the occupants' names: Dr Gibarian, Dr Snow, Dr Sartorius. On the fourth, there was no nameplate. I hesitated, then pressed the handle down gently and slowly opened the door. As I did so, I had a premonition, amounting almost to a certainty, that there was someone inside. I went in.

There was no one. Another wide panoramic window, almost as large as the one in the cabin where I had found Snow, overhung the ocean, which, sunlit on this side, shone with an oleaginous gleam, as though the waves secreted a reddish oil. A crimson glow pervaded the whole room, whose layout suggested a ship's cabin. On one side, flanked by book-filled shelves, a retractable bed stood against the wall. On the other, between the numerous lockers, hung nickel frames enclosing a series of aerial photographs stuck end to end with adhesive tape, and racks full of test-tubes and retorts plugged with cotton-wool. Two tiers of white enamel boxes took up the space beneath the window. I lifted some of the lids; the boxes were crammed with all kinds of instruments, intertwined with plastic tubing. The corners of

12

the room were occupied by a refrigerator, a tap and a demisting device. For lack of space on the big table by the window, a microscope stood on the floor. Turning round, I saw a tall locker beside the entrance door. It was half-open, filled with atmosphere suits, laboratory smocks, insulated aprons, underclothing, boots for planetary exploration, and aluminium cylinders: portable oxygen gear. Two sets of this equipment, complete with masks, hung down from one of the knobs of the vertical bed. Everywhere there was the same chaos, a general disorder which someone had made a hasty attempt to disguise. I sniffed the air. I could detect a faint smell of chemical reagents and traces of something more acrid – chlorine? Instinctively I searched the ceiling for the grilles over the air-vents: strips of paper attached to the bars were fluttering gently; the air was circulating normally. In order to make a relatively free space around the bed, between the bookshelves and the locker, I cleared two chairs of their litter of books, instruments and tools, which I piled haphazardly on the other side of the room.

I pulled out a bracket to hang up my spacesuit, took hold of the zip-fastener, then let go again. Deterred by the confused idea that I was depriving myself of a shield, I could not bring myself to remove it. Once more I looked round the room. I checked that the door was shut tight and that it had no lock, and after a brief hesitation I dragged some of the heaviest boxes to the doorway. Having built this temporary barricade, I freed myself from my clanking armour in three quick movements. A narrow looking-glass, built into the locker door, reflected part of the room, and out of the corner of my eye I caught sight of something moving. I jumped, but it was only my own reflection. Underneath the spacesuit, my overalls were drenched with sweat. I took them off and pulled back a sliding door, revealing the bright-tiled walls of a small bathroom. A long, flat box lay in the hollow at the base of the shower; I carried it into the room. As I put it down, the springlid flew up and disclosed a number of com-

partments filled with strange objects: misshapen forms in a
dark metal, grotesque replicas of the instruments in the
racks. Not one of the tools was usable; they were blunted,
distorted, melted, as though they had been in a furnace.
Strangest of all, even the porcelain handles, virtually
incombustible, were twisted out of shape. Even at maximum
temperature, no laboratory furnace could have melted them;
only, perhaps, an atomic pile. I took a Geiger counter from
the pocket on my spacesuit, but when I held it over the debris, it remained dumb.

By now I was wearing nothing but my underwear. I tore it
off, flung it across the room and dashed under the shower.
The shock of the water did me good. Turning beneath the
scalding, needle-sharp jets, I scrubbed myself vigorously,
splashing the walls, expelling, eradicating from my skin the
thick scum of morbid apprehensions which had pervaded
me since my arrival.

I rummaged in the locker and found a work-suit which
could also be worn under an atmosphere suit. As I pocketed
my few belongings, I felt something hard tucked between
the pages of my notebook: it was a key, the key to my apart-
ment, down there on Earth. Absently, I turned it over in my
fingers. Finally I put it down on the table. It occurred to me
suddenly that I might need a weapon. An all-purpose
pocket-knife was hardly sufficient for my needs, but I had
nothing else, and I was not going to start searching for a
gamma pistol or something else of the kind.

I sat down on a tubular stool in the middle of the clear
space, glad to be alone, and seeing with satisfaction that I
had over half an hour to myself. (By nature, I have always
been scrupulous about keeping engagements, whether
important or trivial.) The hands of the clock, its face divided
into twenty-four hours, pointed to seven o'clock. The sun
was setting. 07.00 hours here was 20.00 hours on board the
Prometheus. On Moddard's screens, Solaris would be nothing
but an indistinct dust-cloud, mingled with the stars. But

what did the *Prometheus* matter to me now? I closed my eyes. I could hear no sound except the moaning of the ventilation pipes and a faint trickling of water from the bathroom.

If I had understood correctly, it was only a short time since Gibarian had died. What had they done with his body? Had they buried it? No, that was impossible on this planet. I puzzled over the question for a long time, concentrating on the fate of the corpse; then, realizing the absurdity of my thoughts, I began to pace up and down. My toe knocked against a canvas bag half-buried under a pile of books; I bent down and picked it up. It contained a small bottle made of coloured glass, so light that it might have been blown out of paper. I held it up to the window in the purplish glow of the sombre twilight, now overhung by a sooty fog. What was I doing, allowing myself to be distracted by irrelevancies, by the first trifle which came to hand?

I gave a start: the lights had gone on, activated by a photo-electric relay; the sun had set. What would happen next? I was so tense that the sensation of an empty space behind me became unbearable. In an attempt to pull myself together, I took a chair over to the bookshelves and chose a book familiar to me: the second volume of the early monograph by Hughes and Eugel, *Historia Solaris*. I rested the thick, solidly bound volume on my knees and began leafing through the pages.

The discovery of Solaris dated from about one hundred years before I was born.

The planet orbits two suns: a red sun and a blue sun. For forty-five years after its discovery, no spacecraft had visited Solaris. At that time, the Gamow-Shapley theory – that life was impossible on planets which are satellites of two solar bodies – was firmly believed. The orbit is constantly being modified by variations in the gravitational pull in the course of its revolutions around the two suns.

Due to these fluctuations in gravity, the orbit is either flattened or distended and the elements of life, if they appear, are inevitably destroyed, either by intense heat or an extreme drop in temperature. These changes take place at intervals estimated in millions of years – very short intervals, that is, according to the laws of astronomy and biology (evolution takes hundreds of millions of years if not a billion).

According to the earliest calculations, in 500,000 years' time Solaris would be drawn one half of an astronomic unit nearer to its red sun, and a million years after that would be engulfed by the incandescent star.

A few decades later, however, observations seemed to suggest that the planet's orbit was in no way subject to the expected variations: it was stable, as stable as the orbit of the planets in our own solar system.

The observations and calculations were reworked with great precision; they simply confirmed the original conclusions: Solaris's orbit was unstable.

A modest item among the hundreds of planets discovered annually – to which official statistics devoted only a few lines defining the characteristics of their orbits – Solaris eventually began to attract special attention and attain a high rank.

Four years after this promotion, overflying the planet with the *Laakon* and two auxiliary craft, the Ottenskjöld expedition undertook a study of Solaris. This expedition being in the nature of a preliminary, not to say improvised reconnaissance, the scientists were not equipped for a landing. Ottenskjöld placed a quantity of automatic observation satellites into equatorial and polar orbit, their principal function being to measure the gravitational pull. In addition, a study was made of the planet's surface, which is covered by an ocean dotted with innumerable flat, low-lying islands whose combined area is less than that of Europe, although the diameter of Solaris is a fifth greater than Earth's. These expanses of barren, rocky territory, irregularly distributed, are largely concentrated in the southern hemisphere. At the same time the composition of the atmosphere – devoid of oxygen – was analysed, and precise measurements made of the planet's density, from which its albedo and other astronomical characteristics were determined. As was foreseeable, no trace of life was discovered, either on the islands or in the ocean.

During the following ten years, Solaris became the centre of attraction for all observatories concerned with the study of this region of space, for the planet had in the meantime shown the astonishing faculty of maintaining an orbit which ought, without any shadow of doubt, to have been unstable. The problem almost developed into a scandal: since the results of the observations could only be inaccurate, attempts were made (in the interests of science) to denounce and discredit various scientists or else the computers they used.

Lack of funds delayed the departure of a proper Solaris expedition for three years. Finally Shannahan assembled his team and obtained three C-tonnage vessels from the Institute, the largest starships of the period. A year and a half before the arrival of the expedition, which left from the region of Alpha in Aquarius, a second exploration fleet, acting in the name of the Institute, placed an automatic satellite – Luna 247 – into orbit around Solaris. This satellite, after three successive reconstructions at roughly ten-year intervals, is still functioning today. The data it supplied confirmed beyond doubt the findings of the Ottenskjöld expedition concerning the active character of the ocean's movements.

One of Shannahan's ships remained in orbit, while the two others, after some preliminary attempts, landed in the southern hemisphere, in a rocky area about 600 miles square. The work of the expedition lasted eighteen months and was carried out under favourable conditions, apart from an unfortunate accident brought about by the malfunction of some apparatus. In the meantime, the scientists had split into two opposing camps; the bone of contention was the ocean.

17

On the basis of the analyses, it had been accepted that the ocean was an organic formation (at that time, no one had yet dared to call it living). But, while the biologists considered it as a primitive formation – a sort of gigantic entity, a fluid cell, unique and monstrous (which they called 'prebiological'), surrounding the globe with a colloidal envelope several miles thick in places – the astronomers and physicists asserted that it must be an organic structure, extraordinarily evolved. According to them, the ocean possibly exceeded terrestrial organic structures in complexity, since it was capable of exerting an active influence on the planet's orbital path. Certainly, no other factor could be found that might explain the behaviour of Solaris; moreover, the planetophysicists had established a relationship between certain processes of the plasmic ocean and the local measurements of gravitational pull, which altered according to the 'matter transformations' of the ocean.

Consequently it was the physicists, rather than the biologists, who put forward the paradoxical formulation of a 'plasmic mechanism', implying by this a structure, possibly without life as we conceive it, but capable of performing functional activities – on an astronomic scale, it should be emphasized.

It was during this quarrel, whose reverberations soon reached the ears of the most eminent authorities, that the Gamow-Shapley doctrine, unchallenged for eighty years, was shaken for the first time.

There were some who continued to support the Gamow-Shapley contentions, to the effect that the ocean had nothing to do with life, that it was neither 'parabiological' nor 'prebiological' but a geological formation – of extreme rarity, it is true – with the unique ability to stabilize the orbit of Solaris, despite the variations in the forces of attraction. Le Chatelier's law was enlisted in support of this argument.

To challenge this conservative attitude, new hypotheses were advanced – of which Civito-Vitta's was one of the most elaborate – proclaiming that the ocean was the product of a dialectical development: on the basis of its earliest pre-oceanic form, a solution of slow-reacting chemical elements, and by the force of circumstances (the threat to its existence from the changes of orbit), it had reached in a single bound the stage of 'homeostatic ocean', without passing through all the stages of terrestrial evolution, bypassing the unicellular and multicellular phases, the vegetable and the animal, the development of a nervous and cerebral system. In other words, unlike terrestrial organisms, it had not taken hundreds of millions of years to adapt itself to its environment – culminating in the first representatives of a species endowed with reason – but dominated its environment immediately.

This was an original point of view. Nevertheless, the means whereby this colloidal envelope was able to stabilize the planet's orbit remained unknown. For almost a century, devices had existed capable of creating artificial magnetic and gravitational fields; they were called gravitors. But no one could even guess how this formless glue could produce an effect which the gravitors achieved by the use of complicated nuclear reactions and enormously high temperatures. The newspapers of the day, exciting the curiosity of the layman and the anger of the scientist, were full of the most improbable embroideries on the theme of the 'Solaris Mystery', one reporter going so far as to suggest that the ocean was, no less, a distant relation to our electric eels!

Just when a measure of success had been achieved in unravelling this problem, it turned out, as often happened subsequently in the field of Solarist studies, that the explanation replaced one enigma with another, perhaps even more baffling.

Observations showed, at least, that the ocean did not react according to the same principles as our gravitors (which, in any case, would have been impossible), but succeeded in controlling the orbital periodicity directly. One result, among others, was the discovery of discrepancies in the measurement of time along one and the same meridian on Solaris. Thus the ocean was not only in a sense 'aware' of the Einstein-Boëvia theory; it was also capable of exploiting the implications of the latter (which was more than we could say of ourselves).

With the publication of this hypothesis, the scientific world was torn by one of the most violent controversies of the century. Revered and universally accepted theories foundered; the specialist literature was swamped by outrageous and heretical treatises; 'sentient ocean' or 'gravity-controlling colloid' – the debate became a burning issue.

All this happened several years before I was born. When I was a student – new data having accumulated in the meantime – it was already generally agreed that there was life on Solaris, even if it was limited to a single inhabitant.

The second volume of Hughes and Eugel, which I was still leafing through mechanically, began with a systematization that was as ingenious as it was amusing. The table of classification comprised three definitions: Type: Polythera; Class: Syncytialia; Category: Metamorph.

It might have been thought that we knew of an infinite number of examples of the species, whereas in reality there was only the one – weighing, it is true, some 700 billion tons.

Multicoloured illustrations, picturesque graphs, analytical summaries and spectral diagrams flickered through my fingers, explaining the type and rhythm of the fundamental transformations as well as the chemical reactions. Rapidly, infallibly, the thick tome led the reader on to the solid ground of mathematical certitude. One might have assumed that we knew everything there was to be known about this representative of the category Metamorph, which lay some hundreds of metres below the metal hull of the Station, obscured at the moment by the shadows of the four-hour night.

In fact, by no means everybody was yet convinced that the

ocean was actually a living 'creature', and still less, it goes without saying, a rational one. I put the heavy volume back on the shelf and took up the one next to it, which was in two parts. The first part was devoted to a résumé of the countless attempts to establish contact with the ocean. I could well remember how, when I was a student, these attempts were the subject of endless anecdotes, jokes and witticisms. Compared with the proliferation of speculative ideas which were triggered off by this problem, medieval scholasticism seemed a model of scientific enlightenment. The second part, nearly 1500 pages long, was devoted exclusively to the bibliography of the subject. There would not have been enough room for the books themselves in the cabin in which I was sitting.

The first attempts at contact were by means of specially designed electronic apparatus. The ocean itself took an active part in these operations by remodelling the instruments. All this, however, remained somewhat obscure. What exactly did the ocean's 'participation' consist of? It modified certain elements in the submerged instruments, as a result of which the normal discharge frequency was completely disrupted and the recording instruments registered a profusion of signals – fragmentary indications of some outlandish activity, which in fact defeated all attempts at analysis. Did these data point to a momentary condition of stimulation, or to regular impulses correlated with the gigantic structures which the ocean was in the process of creating elsewhere, at the antipodes of the region under investigation? Had the electronic apparatus recorded the cryptic manifestation of the ocean's ancient secrets? Had it revealed its innermost workings to us? Who could tell? No two reactions to the stimuli were the same. Sometimes the instruments almost exploded under the violence of the impulses, sometimes there was total silence; it was impossible to obtain a repetition of any previously observed phenomenon. Constantly, it seemed, the experts were on the brink of deciphering the ever-growing mass of information. Was it not, after all, with this object in mind that computers had been built of virtually limitless capacity, such as no previous problem had ever demanded?

And, indeed, some results *were* obtained. The ocean as a source of electric and magnetic impulses and of gravitation expressed itself in a more or less mathematical language. Also, by calling on the most abstruse branches of statistical analysis, it was possible to classify certain frequencies in the discharges of current. Structural homologues were discovered, not unlike those already observed by physicists in that sector of science which deals with the reciprocal interaction of energy and matter, elements and compounds, the finite and the infinite. This correspondence convinced the scientists that they were confronted with a monstrous entity endowed with reason, a protoplasmic ocean-brain enveloping the entire planet and idling its time away in extravagant theoretical cognitation about the nature of the universe. Our instruments had intercepted minute random fragments of a prodigious and everlasting monologue unfolding in the depths of this colossal brain, which was inevitably beyond our understanding.

So much for the mathematicians. These hypotheses, according to some people, underestimated the resources of the human mind; they bowed to the unknown, proclaiming the ancient doctrine, arrogantly resurrected, of *ignoramus et ignorabimus*. Others regarded the mathematicians' hypotheses as sterile and dangerous nonsense, contributing towards the creation of a modern mythology based on the notion of this giant brain – whether plasmic or electronic was immaterial – as the ultimate objective of existence, the very synthesis of life.

Yet others . . . but the would-be experts were legion and each had his own theory. A comparison of the 'contact' school of thought with other branches of Solarist studies, in which specialization had rapidly developed, especially during the last quarter of a century, made it clear that a Solarist-cybernetician had difficulty in making himself understood to a Solarist-symmetriadologist. Veubeke, director of the Institute when I was studying there, had asked jokingly one day: 'How do you expect to communicate with the ocean, when you can't even understand one another?' The jest contained more than a grain of truth.

The decision to categorize the ocean as a metamorph was not an arbitrary one. Its undulating surface was capable of generating extremely diverse formations which resembled nothing ever seen on Earth, and the function of these sudden eruptions of plasmic 'creativity', whether adaptive, explorative or what, remained an enigma.

Lifting the heavy volume with both hands, I replaced it on the shelf, and thought to myself that our scholarship, all the information accumulated in the libraries, amounted to a useless jumble of words, a sludge of statements and suppositions, and that we had not progressed an inch in the seventy-eight years since researches had begun. The situation seemed much worse now than in the time of the pioneers, since the assiduous efforts of so many years had not resulted in a single indisputable conclusion.

The sum total of known facts was strictly negative. The ocean did not use machines, even though in certain circumstances it seemed capable of creating them. During the first two years of exploratory work, it had reproduced elements of some of the submerged instruments. Thereafter, it simply ignored the experiments we went on pursuing, as though it had lost all interest in our instruments and our activities – as though, indeed, it was no longer interested in us. It did not possess a nervous system (to go on with the inventory of 'negative knowledge') or cells, and its structure was not proteiform. It did not always react even to the most powerful stimuli (it ignored completely, for example, the catastrophic accident which occurred during the second Giese expedition: an auxiliary rocket, falling from a height of 300,000 metres, crashed on the planet's surface and the radioactive explosion of its nuclear reserves destroyed the plasma within a radius of 2500 metres).

Gradually, in scientific circles, the 'Solaris Affair' came to be regarded as a lost cause, notably among the administrators of the Institute, where voices had recently been raised suggesting that financial support should be withdrawn and research suspended. No one, until then, had dared to suggest the final liquidation of the Station; such a decision would have smacked too obviously of defeat. But in the course of semi-official discussions a number of scientists recommended an 'honourable' withdrawal from Solaris.

Many people in the world of science, however, especially among the young, had unconsciously come to regard the 'affair' as a touchstone of individual values. All things considered, they claimed, it was not simply a question of penetrating Solarist civilization, it was essentially a test of ourselves, of the limitations of human knowledge. For some time, there was a widely held notion (zealously fostered by the daily press) to the effect that the 'thinking ocean' of Solaris was a gigantic brain, prodigiously well developed and several million years in advance of our own civilization, a sort of 'cosmic yogi', a sage, a symbol of omniscience, which had long ago understood the vanity of all action and for this reason had retreated into an unbreakable silence. The notion was incorrect, for the living ocean was active. Not, it is true, according to human ideas – it did not build cities or bridges, nor did it manufacture flying machines. It did not try to reduce distances, nor was it concerned with the conquest of Space (the ultimate criterion, some people thought, of man's superiority). But it was engaged in a never-ending process of transformation, an 'ontological autometamorphosis'. (There were any amount of scientific neologisms in accounts of Solarist activities.) Moreover, any scientist who devotes himself to the study of Solariana has the indelible impression that he can discern fragments of an intelligent

24

structure, perhaps endowed with genius, haphazardly mingled with outlandish phenomena, apparently the product of
an unhinged mind. Thus was born the conception of the
'autistic ocean' as opposed to the 'ocean-yogi'.

These hypotheses resurrected one of the most ancient of
philosophical problems: the relation between matter and
mind, and between mind and consciousness. Du Haart was
the first to have the audacity to maintain that the ocean possessed a consciousness. The problem, which the method-
ologists hastened to dub metaphysical, provoked all kinds of
arguments and discussions. Was it possible for thought to
exist without consciousness? Could one, in any case, apply
the word thought to the processes observed in the ocean? Is a
mountain only a huge stone? Is a planet an enormous mountain? Whatever the terminology, the new scale of size introduced new norms and new phenomena.

The question appeared as a contemporary version of the
problem of squaring the circle. Every independent thinker
endeavoured to register his personal contribution to the hoard
of Solarist studies. New theories proliferated: the ocean was
evidence of a state of degeneration, of regression, following a
phase of 'intellectual repletion'; it was a deviant neoplasm,
the product of the bodies of former inhabitants of the planet,
whom it had devoured, swallowed up, dissolving and
blending the residue into this unchanging, self-propagating
form, supracellular in structure.

By the white light of the fluorescent tubes – a pale imitation of terrestrial daylight – I cleared the table of its clutter of
apparatus and books. Arms outstretched and my hands
gripping the chromium edging, I unrolled a map of Solaris
on the plastic surface and studied it at length. The living
ocean had its peaks and its canyons. Its islands, which were
covered with a decomposing mineral deposit, were certainly
related to the nature of the ocean bed. But did it control the
eruption and subsidence of the rocky formations buried in
its depths? No one knew. Gazing at the big flat projection of

the two hemispheres, coloured in various tones of blue and purple, I experienced once again that thrill of wonder which had so often gripped me, and which I had felt as a schoolboy on learning of the existence of Solaris for the first time.

Lost in contemplation of this bewildering map, my mind in a daze, I temporarily forgot the mystery surrounding Gibarian's death and the uncertainty of my own future.

The different sections of the ocean were named after the scientists who had explored them. I was examining Thexall's swell, which surrounded the equatorial archipelagos, when I had a sudden sensation of being watched.

I was still leaning over the map, but I no longer saw it; my limbs were in the grip of a sort of paralysis. The crates and a small locker still barricaded the door, which was in front of me. It's only a robot, I told myself – yet I had not discovered any in the room and none could have entered without my knowledge. My back and my neck seemed to be on fire; the sensation of this relentless, fixed stare was becoming unbearable. With my head shrinking between my hunched shoulders, I leant harder and harder against the table, until it began slowly to slide away. The movement released me; I spun round.

The room was empty. There was nothing in front of me except the wide convex window and, beyond it, the night. But the same sensation persisted. The night stared me in the face, amorphous, blind, infinite, without frontiers. Not a single star relieved the darkness behind the glass. I pulled the thick curtains. I had been in the Station less than an hour, yet already I was showing signs of morbidity. Was it the effect of Gibarian's death? In so far as I knew him, I had imagined that nothing could shake his nerve: now, I was no longer so sure.

I stood in the middle of the room, beside the table. My breathing became more regular, I felt the sweat chill on my forehead. What was it I had been thinking about a moment ago? Ah, yes, robots! It was surprising that I had not come across one anywhere on the Station. What could have become of them all? The only one with which I had been in contact – at a distance – belonged to the vehicle reception services. But what about the others?

I looked at my watch. It was time to rejoin Snow.

I left the room. The dome was feebly lit by luminous filaments running the length of the ceiling. I went up to Gibarian's door and stood there, motionless. There was total silence. I gripped the handle. I had in fact no intention of going in, but the handle went down and the door opened, disclosing a chink of darkness. The lights went on. In one quick movement, I entered and silently closed the door behind me. Then I turned round.

My shoulders brushed against the door panels. The room was larger than mine. A curtain decorated with little pink and blue flowers (not regulation Station equipment, but no doubt brought from Earth with his personal belongings) covered three-quarters of the panoramic window. Around the walls were bookshelves and cupboards, painted pale green with silvery highlights. Both shelves and cupboards had been emptied of their contents, which were piled into heaps, among the furniture. At my feet, blocking the way, were two overturned trolleys buried beneath a heap of periodicals spilling out of bulging briefcases which had burst open. Books with their pages splayed out fanwise were stained with coloured liquids which had spilt from broken retorts and bottles with corroded stoppers, receptacles made of such thick glass that a single fall, even from a considerable height, could not have shattered them in such a way. Beneath the window lay an overturned desk, an anglepoise lamp crumpled underneath it; two legs of an upturned stool were stuck in the half-open drawers. A flood of papers of every conceivable size swamped the floor. My interest quickened as I recognized Gibarian's handwriting. As I stooped to gather together the loose sheets, I noticed that my hand was casting a double shadow.

I straightened up. The pink curtain glowed brightly, traversed by a streak of incandescent, steely-blue light which was gradually widening. I pulled the curtain aside. An unbearable glare extended along the horizon, chasing before it an army of spectral shadows, which rose up from among the waves and dispersed in the direction of the Station. It was the dawn. After an hour of darkness the planet's second sun – the blue sun – was rising in the sky.

The automatic switch cut off the lights as I returned to the heap of papers. The first thing I came across was a detailed description of an experiment, evidently decided upon three weeks before. Gibarian had planned to expose the plasma to an intensive bombardment of X-rays. I gathered from the context that the paper was addressed to Sartorius, whose job it was to organize operations. What I was holding in my hand was a copy of the plan.

The whiteness of the paper hurt my eyes. This new day was different from the previous one. In the warm glow of the red sun, mists overhung a black ocean with blood-red reflections, and waves, clouds and sky were almost constantly veiled in a crimson haze. Now, the blue sun pierced the flower-printed curtain with a crystalline light. My sun-tanned hands looked grey. The room had changed; all the red-reflecting objects had lost their lustre and had turned a greyish-brown, whereas those which were white, green and yellow had acquired a vivid brilliance and seemed to give off their own light. Screwing up my eyes, I risked another glance through a chink in the curtain: an expanse of molten metal trembled and shimmered under a white-hot sky. I shut my eyes and drew back. On the shelf above the washbasin (which had recently been badly chipped) I found a pair of dark glasses, so big that when I put them on they covered half my face. The curtain appeared to glow with a sodium light. I went on reading, picking up the sheets of paper and arranging them on the only usable table. There were gaps in the text, and I searched in vain for the missing pages.

I came across a report of experiments already carried out, and learnt that, for four days running, Gibarian and Sartorius had submitted the ocean to radiation at a point 1400 miles from the present position of the Station. The use of X-rays was banned by a UN convention, because of their harmful effects, and I was certain that no one had sent a request to Earth for authorization to proceed with such experiments.

Looking up, I caught sight of my face in the mirror of a half-open locker door: masked by the dark glasses, it was deathly pale. The room, too, glinting with blue and white reflections, looked equally bizarre; but soon there came a prolonged screech of metal as the air-tight outer shutters slid across the window. There was an instant of darkness, and then the lights came on; they seemed to me to be curiously dim. It grew hotter and hotter. The regular drone of the air-conditioning was now a high-pitched whine: the Station's refrigeration plant was running at full capacity. Nevertheless, the overpowering heat grew more and more intense.

I heard footsteps. Someone was walking through the dome. In two silent strides, I reached the door. The footsteps slowed down; whoever it was was behind it. The handle moved. Automatically, without thinking, I gripped it. The pressure did not increase, but nor did it relax. Neither of us, on either side of the door, said a word. We remained there, motionless, each of us holding the handle. Suddenly it straightened up again, freeing itself from my grasp. The muffled footsteps receded. With my ear glued to the panel, I went on listening. I heard nothing more.

The Visitors

I hastily pocketed Gibarian's notes and went over to the locker. Work-suits and clothes had been pushed to one side as though someone had hidden himself at the back. On the floor I saw the corner of an envelope sticking out from a heap of papers and picked it up. It was addressed to me. Dry-mouthed with apprehension, I tore it open; I had to force myself to unfold the note inside.

In his even handwriting, small but perfectly legible, Gibarian had written two lines:

Supplement Dir. Solar. Vol. 1: Vot. Separat.

Messenger ds aff. F.; Ravintzer: The Little Apocrypha.

That was all, not another word. Did these two lines contain some vital piece of information? When had he written them? I told myself that the first thing to do was to consult the library index. I knew the supplement to the first volume of the annual of Solarist studies; or rather, without having read it, I knew of its existence – but was it not a document of purely historical interest? As for Ravintzer and *The Little Apocrypha*, I had never heard of them.

What next?

I was already a quarter of an hour late for my meeting with Snow. With my back to the door, I looked the room over carefully once more. Only then did I notice the bed standing up against the wall, half concealed by a large map of Solaris. Something was hanging down behind the map; it was a pocket tape-recorder, and I noted that nine-tenths of the tape had been used. I took the machine out of its case (which I hung back where I had found it) and slipped it into my pocket.

Before leaving, I listened intently with my eyes closed.

There was no sound from outside. I opened the door on to a yawning gulf of darkness – until it occurred to me to remove my dark glasses. The dome was feebly lit by the glowing filaments in the ceiling.

A number of corridors spread out in a star-shaped pattern between the four doors of the sleeping quarters and the narrow passage leading to the radio-cabin. Suddenly, looming up in the opening which led to the communal bathroom, a tall silhouette appeared, barely distinguishable in the surrounding gloom. I stood stock still, frozen to the spot. A giant Negress was coming silently towards me with a smooth, rolling gait. I caught a gleam from the whites of her eyes and heard the soft slapping of her bare feet. She was wearing nothing but a yellow skirt of plaited straw; her enormous breasts swung freely and her black arms were as thick as thighs. Less than a yard separated us as she passed me, but she did not give me so much as a glance. She went on her way, her grass skirt swinging rhythmically, resembling one of those steatopygous statues in anthropological museums. She opened Gibarian's door and on the threshold her silhouette stood out distinctly against the bright light from inside the room. Then she closed the door behind her and I was alone.

Terror-stricken, I stared blankly round the big, empty hall. What had happened? What had I seen? Suddenly, my mind reeled as I recalled Snow's warnings. Who was this monstrous Aphrodite? I took a step, a single pace, in the direction of Gibarian's room, but I knew perfectly well that I would not go in.

I do not know how long I remained leaning against the cool metal wall, hearing nothing except the distant, monotonous whine of the air-conditioners. Eventually I pulled myself together and made my way to the radio-cabin. As I pressed down the door handle, I heard a harsh voice:

'Who's there?'

'It's me, Kelvin.'

Snow was seated at a table between a pile of aluminium crates and the transmitter, eating meat concentrate straight out of a tin. Did he then never leave the place? Dazedly, I watched him chewing until I realized that I, too, was famished. I went to a cupboard, selected the least dusty plate I could find, and sat down opposite Snow. We ate in silence.

Snow got up, uncorked a vacuum flask and filled two tumblers with clear, hot soup. Then he put the flask down on the floor; there was no room on the table.

'Have you seen Sartorius?' he asked.

'No. Where is he?'

'Upstairs.'

Upstairs: that meant the laboratory. We finished our meal without exchanging another word, Snow dutifully scraping the bottom of his tin. The outer shutter was in place over the window and reflections from the four ceiling lights gleamed on the laminated surface of the transmitter. Snow had put on a loose black sweater, frayed at the wrists. The taut skin over his cheekbones was marbled with tiny blood-vessels.

'What's the matter?' he asked.

'Nothing, why?'

'You're pouring with sweat.'

I wiped my forehead. It was true, I was dripping wet; it must have been reaction, after my unexpected encounter. Snow gave me a questioning glance. Should I tell him? If only he had taken me into his confidence . . . What incomprehensible game was being played here, and who was whose enemy?

'It's hot. I should have expected your air-conditioning to work better than this!'

'It adjusts itself automatically every hour.' He looked at me closely. 'Are you sure it's only the heat?'

I did not answer. He tossed the utensils and the empty tins into the sink, returned to his armchair and went on with his interrogation.

'What are your plans?'

'That depends on you,' I answered coolly. 'I suppose you have a research programme? A new stimulus, X-rays, that sort of thing . . .'

He frowned.

'X-rays? Who's been talking to you about that?'

'I don't remember. Someone dropped a hint – on the *Prometheus* perhaps. Why, have you begun?'

'I don't know the details, it was an idea of Gibarian's. He and Sartorius set it up together. I wonder how you could have heard of it.'

I shrugged my shoulders.

'Funny that you shouldn't know the details. You ought to, since you're the one who . . .'

I left the sentence unfinished; Snow said nothing.

The whining of the air-conditioners had stopped. The temperature stayed at a bearable level, but a high-pitched drone persisted, like the buzzing of a dying insect.

Snow got up from his chair and leant over the console of the transmitter. He began to press knobs at random, and to no effect, since he had left the activating switch off. He went on fidgeting with them for a moment, then he remarked:

'There are certain formalities to be dealt with concerning . . .'

'Yes?' I prompted, to his back.

He turned round and gave me a hostile look. Involuntarily, I had annoyed him; but ignorant of the role he was playing, I could only wait and see. His Adam's apple rose and fell inside the collar of his sweater:

'You've been into Gibarian's room,' he blurted out accusingly.

I looked at him calmly.

'You *have* been in there, haven't you?'

'If you say so . . .'

'Was there anyone there?'

So he had seen her, or, at least, knew of her existence!

'No, no one. Who could there have been?'

'Why didn't you let me in, then?'

'Because I was afraid. I thought of your warnings and when the handle moved, I automatically hung on to it. Why didn't you say it was you? I would have let you in.'

'I thought it was Sartorius,' he answered, in a faltering voice.

'And suppose it had been?'

Once again, he parried my question with one of his own.

'What do you think happened in there?'

I hesitated.

'You're the one who should know. Where is he?'

'Gibarian? In the cold store. We took him there straight away this morning, after we'd found him in the locker.'

'The locker? Was he dead?'

'His heart was still beating, but he had stopped breathing.'

'Did you try resuscitation?'

'No.'

'Why not?'

'I didn't have the chance,' he mumbled. 'By the time I'd moved him, he was dead.'

Snow picked up a sheet of paper from the fitted desk in the corner and held it out to me.

'I have drafted a post-mortem report. I'm not sorry you've seen the room, as a matter of fact. Cause of death – pernostal injection, lethal dose. It's all here . . .'

I ran my eyes over the paper, and murmured:

'Suicide? For what reason?'

'Nervous troubles, depression, call it what you like. You know more about that sort of thing than I do.'

I was still seated; Snow was standing over me.

Looking him in the eye, I said:

'I only know what I've seen for myself.'

'What are you trying to say?' he asked calmly.

'He injected himself with pernostal and hid in the locker, right? In that case, it's not a question of nervous troubles or a fit of depression, but of a very serious paranoid condition.'

Speaking more and more deliberately and continuing to look him in the eyes, I added: 'What is certain is that he thought he saw something.'

Snow began fiddling with the transmitter again.

After a moment's silence, I went on.

'Your signature's here. What about Sartorius's?'

'As I told you, he's in the laboratory. He never shows his face. I suppose he's . . .'

'What?'

'Locked himself in.'

'Locked himself in? I see . . . you mean he's barricaded himself in?'

'Possibly.'

'Snow, there's someone on the Station. Someone apart from us.'

He had stopped playing with the knobs and was leaning sideways, staring at me.

'You've seen it!'

'You warned me. Against what? Against whom? A hallucination?'

'What did you see?'

'Shall we say . . . a human being?'

He remained silent. Turning his back as though to hide his face from me, he tapped the metal plating with his finger-tips. I looked at his hands; there was no longer any trace of blood between the fingers. I had a brief moment of dizziness.

In scarcely more than a whisper, as though I were imparting a secret and afraid of being overheard, I said:

'It's not a mirage, is it? It's a real person, someone you can touch, someone you can . . . draw blood from. And what's more, someone you've seen only today.'

'How do you know?'

He had not moved; his face was still obstinately turned to the wall and I was addressing his back.

'It was before I arrived, just before I arrived, wasn't it?'

35

His whole body contracted, and I could see his panic-stricken expression.

'What about you?' he said in a strangled voice. 'Who are you?'

I thought he was about to attack me. It was not at all the reaction I had expected. The situation was becoming grotesque. Obviously, he did not believe that I was who I claimed to be. But what could this mean? He was becoming more and more terrified of me. Was he delirious? Could he have been affected by unfiltered gases from the planet's atmosphere? Anything seemed possible. And then again, I too had seen this . . . creature, so what about me?

'Who is she?' I asked.

These words reassured him. For a moment, he looked at me searchingly, as though he was still doubtful of me; then he collapsed into his chair and put his head in his hands. Even before he opened his mouth, I knew that he had still not made up his mind to give me a direct answer.

'I'm worn out,' he said weakly.

'Who is she?' I insisted.

'If you don't know . . . '

'Go on, know what?'

'Nothing.'

'Listen, Snow! We are isolated, completely cut off. Let's put our cards on the table. Things are confused enough as it is. You've got to tell me what you know!'

'What about you?' he retorted, suspiciously.

'All right, I'll tell you and then you tell me. Don't worry, I shan't think you're mad.'

'Mad! Good God!' He tried to smile. 'But you haven't understood a thing, not a single thing. He never for one moment thought that he was mad. If he had he would never have done it. He would still be alive.'

'In other words, your report, this business of nervous troubles, is a fabrication.'

'Of course.'

'Why not write the truth?'

'Why?' he repeated.

A long silence followed. It was true that I was still completely in the dark. I had been under the impression that I had overcome his doubts and that we were going to pool our resources to solve the enigma. Why, then, was he refusing to talk?

'Where are the robots?'

'In the store-rooms. We've locked them all away; only the reception robots are operational.'

'Why?'

Once more, he refused to answer.

'You don't want to talk about it?'

'I can't.'

He seemed constantly on the point of unburdening himself, only to pull himself up at the last moment. Perhaps I would do better to tackle Sartorius. Then I remembered the letter and, as I thought of it, realized how important it was.

'Do you intend continuing with the experiments?'

He gave a contemptuous shrug:

'What good would that do?'

'Oh – in that case, what do *you* suggest we do?'

He was silent. In the distance, there was a faint noise of bare feet padding over the floor. The muffled echo of these shuffling steps reverberated eerily among the nickel-plated and laminated equipment and the tall shafts, furrowed with glass tubes, which encased the complicated electronic installations.

Unable to control myself any longer, I stood up. As I listened to the approaching footsteps, I watched Snow. Behind the drooping lids, his eyes showed no fear. Was he not afraid of her, then?

'Where does she come from?' I asked.

'I don't know.'

The sound of the footsteps faded, then died away.

'Don't you believe me?' he said. 'I swear to you that I don't know.'

In the silence that followed, I opened a locker, pushed the clumsy atmosphere suits aside and found, as I expected, hanging at the back, the gas pistols used for manoeuvring in space. I took one out, checked the charge, and slung the harness over my shoulder. It was not, strictly speaking, a weapon, but it was better than nothing.

As I was adjusting a strap, Snow showed his yellow teeth in a mocking grin.

'Good hunting!' he said.

I turned towards the door.

'Thanks.'

He dragged himself out of his chair.

'Kelvin!'

I looked at him. He was no longer smiling. I have never seen such an expression of weariness on anyone's face.

He mumbled:

'Kelvin, it isn't that . . . Really, I . . . I can't . . .'

I waited; his lips moved, but uttered no sound. I turned on my heel and went out.

Sartorius

I followed a long, empty corridor, then forked right. I had never lived on the Station, but during my training on Earth I had spent six weeks in an exact replica of it; when I reached a short aluminium stairway, I knew where it led.

The library was in darkness, and I had to fumble for the light switch. I first consulted the index, then dialled the coordinates for the first volume of the *Solarist Annual* and its supplement. A red light came on. I turned to the register: the two books were marked out to Gibarian, together with *The Little Apocrypha*. I switched the lights off and returned to the lower deck.

In spite of having heard the footsteps receding, I was afraid to re-enter Gibarian's room. *She* might return. I hesitated for some time outside the door; finally, pressing down the handle, I forced myself to go in.

There was no one in the room. I began rummaging through the books scattered beneath the window, interrupting my search only to close the locker door: I could not bear the sight of the empty space among the work-suits.

The supplement was not in the first pile, so, one by one, I started methodically picking up the rest of the books around the room. When I reached the final pile, between the bed and the wardrobe, I found the volume I was looking for.

I was hoping to find some sort of clue and, sure enough, a book-marker had been slipped between the pages of the index. A name, unfamiliar to me, had been underlined in red: André Berton. The corresponding page numbers indicated two different chapters; glancing at the first, I learnt that Berton was a reserve pilot on Shannahan's ship. The second reference appeared about a hundred pages further on.

At first, it seemed, Shannahan's expedition had proceeded with extreme caution. When, however, after sixteen days, the plasmatic ocean had not only shown no signs of aggression, but appeared to shun any direct contact with men and machines, recoiling whenever anything approached its surface, Shannahan and his deputy, Timolis, discontinued some of the precautions which were hindering the progress of their work. The force fences which had been used to demarcate and protect the working areas were taken back to base, and the expedition split up into groups of two or three men, some groups making reconnaissance flights over a radius of several hundred miles.

Apart from some unexpected damage to the oxygen-supply systems – the atmosphere had an unusually corrosive effect on the valves, which had to be replaced almost daily – four days passed without mishap. On the morning of the fifth day – twenty-one days after the arrival of the expedition – two scientists, Carucci and Fechner (the first a radiobiologist, the second a physicist), left on a mission aboard a hovercraft. Six hours later, the explorers were overdue. Timolis, who was in charge of the base in Shannahan's absence, raised the alarm and diverted every available man into search-parties.

By a fatal combination of circumstances, long-range radio contact had been cut that morning an hour after the departure of the exploration groups – a large spot had appeared on the red sun, producing a heavy bombardment of charged particles in the upper atmosphere. Only the ultra-shortwave transmitters continued to function, and contact was restricted to a radius of about twenty miles. As a crowning stroke of bad luck, a thick fog descended just before sunset and the search had to be called off.

The rescue teams were returning to base when the hovercraft was spotted by a flitter, barely twenty-four miles from the command-ship. The engine was running and the machine, at first sight undamaged, was hovering above the waves. Carucci alone could be seen, semi-conscious, in the glass-domed cockpit.

The hovercraft was escorted back to base. After treatment, Carucci quickly regained consciousness, but could throw no light on Fechner's disappearance. Just after they had decided to return to base a valve in his oxygen-gear had failed and a small amount of unfiltered gas had penetrated his atmosphere suit. In an attempt to repair the valve, Fechner had been forced to undo his safety belt and stand up. That was the last thing Carucci could remember.

According to the experts who reconstructed the sequence of events, Fechner must have opened the cabin roof because it impeded his movements – a perfectly legitimate thing to do since the cabins of these vehicles were not air-tight, the glass dome merely providing some protection against infiltration and turbulence. While Fechner was occupied with his colleague, his own oxygen supply had probably been damaged and, no longer realizing what he was doing, he had pulled himself up on to the superstructure, from which he had fallen into the ocean.

Fechner thus became the ocean's first victim. Although the atmosphere suit was buoyant, they searched for his body without success. It was, of course, possible that it was still floating somewhere on the surface, but the expedition was not equipped for a thorough search of this immense, undulating desert, covered with patches of dense fog.

By dusk, all but one of the search craft had returned to base; only a big supply helicopter piloted by André Berton was still missing. Just as they were about to raise the alarm, the aircraft appeared. Berton was obviously suffering from nervous shock; after struggling out of his suit, he ran round in circles like a madman. He had to be overpowered, but went on shouting and sobbing. It was rather surprising behaviour, to put it mildly, on the part of a man who had been flying for seventeen years and was well used to the hazards of cosmic navigation. The doctors assumed that he too was suffering from the effects of unfiltered gases.

Having more or less recovered his senses, Berton nevertheless refused to leave the base, or even to go near the window overlooking the ocean. Two days later, he asked for permission to dictate a flight-report, stressing the importance of what he was about to reveal. This report was studied by the expeditionary council, who concluded that it was the morbid creation of a mind under the influence of poisonous gases from the atmosphere. As for the supposed revelations, they were evidently regarded as part of Berton's clinical history rather than that of the expedition itself, and they were not described.

So much for the supplement. It seemed to me that Berton's report must at any rate provide a key to the mystery. What strange happening could have had such a shattering effect on a veteran space-pilot? I began to search through the books once more, but *The Little Apocrypha* was not to be found. I was growing more and more exhausted and left the room, having decided to postpone the search until the following day.

As I was passing the foot of the stairway, I noticed that the aluminium treads were streaked with light falling from above. Sartorius was still at work. I decided to go up and see him.

It was hotter on the upper deck, but the paper strips still fluttered frenziedly at the air-vents. The corridor was wide and low-ceilinged. The main laboratory was enclosed by a thick panel of opaque glass in a chrome embrasure. A dark curtain screened the door on the inside, and the light was coming from windows let in above the lintel. I pressed down the handle, but, as I expected, the door refused to budge. The only sound from the laboratory was an intermittent whine like that of a defective gas jet. I knocked. No reply. I called:

'Sartorius! Dr Sartorius! I'm the new man, Kelvin. I must see you, it's very important. Please let me in!'

There was a rustling of papers.

'It's me, Kelvin. You must have heard of me. I arrived off the *Prometheus* a few hours ago.'

I was shouting, my lips glued to the angle where the door joined the metal frame.

'Dr. Sartorius, I'm alone. Please open the door!'

Not a word. Then the same rustling as before, followed by the clink of metal instruments on a tray. Then ... I could scarcely believe my ears ... there came a succession of little short footsteps, like the rapid drumming of a pair of tiny feet, or remarkably agile fingers tapping out the rhythm of steps on the lid of an empty tin box.

I yelled:

'Dr. Sartorius, are you going to open this door, yes or no?'

No answer. Nothing but the pattering, and, simultaneously, the sound of a man walking on tiptoe. But, if the man was moving about, he could not at the same time be tapping out an imitation of a child's footsteps.

No longer able to control my growing fury, I burst out:

'Dr. Sartorius, I have not made a sixteen-month journey just to come here and play games! I'll count up to ten. If you don't let me in, I shall break down the door!'

In fact, I was doubtful whether it would be easy to force this particular door, and the discharge of a gas pistol is not very powerful. Nevertheless, I was determined somehow or other to carry out my threat, even if it meant resorting to explosives, which I could probably find in the munition store. I could not draw back now; I could not go on playing an insane game with all the cards stacked against me.

There was the sound of a struggle – or was it simply objects being thrust aside? The curtain was pulled back, and an elongated shadow was projected on to the glass.

A hoarse, high-pitched voice spoke:

'If I open the door, you must give me your word not to come in.'

'In that case, why open it?'

'I'll come out.'

'Very well, I promise.'

The silhouette vanished and the curtain was carefully replaced.

Obscure noises came from inside the laboratory. I heard a scraping – a table being dragged across the floor? At last, the lock clicked back, and the glass panel opened just enough to allow Sartorius to slip through into the corridor.

He stood with his back against the door, very tall and thin, all bones under his white sweater. He had a black scarf knotted around his neck, and over his arm he was carrying a laboratory smock, covered with chemical burns. His head, which was unusually narrow, was cocked to one side. I could not see his eyes: he wore curved dark glasses, which covered up half his face. His lower jaw was elongated; he had bluish lips and enormous, blue-tinged ears. He was unshaven. Red anti-radiation gloves hung by their laces from his wrists.

For a moment we looked at one another with undisguised aversion. His shaggy hair (he had obviously cut it himself) was the colour of lead, his beard grizzled. Like Snow, his forehead was burnt, but the lower half only; above, it was pallid. He must have worn some kind of cap when exposed to the sun.

'Well, I'm listening,' he said.

I had the impression that he did not care what I had to say to him. Standing there, tense, still pressed against the door panel, his attention was mainly directed to what was going on behind him.

Disconcerted, I hardly knew how to begin.

'My name is Kelvin,' I said. 'You must have heard about me. I am, or rather I was, a colleague of Gibarian's.'

His thin face, entirely composed of vertical planes, exactly as I had always imagined Don Quixote's, was quite expressionless. This blank mask did not help me to find the right words.

'I heard that Gibarian was dead . . .' I broke off.

'Yes. Go on, I'm listening.' His voice betrayed his impatience.

'Did he commit suicide? Who found the body, you or Snow?'

'Why ask me? Didn't Dr Snow tell you what happened?'

'I wanted to hear your own account.'

'You've studied psychology, haven't you, Dr Kelvin?'

'Yes. What of it?'

'You think of yourself as a servant of science?'

'Yes, of course. What has that to do with . . .'

'You are not an officer of the law. At this hour of the day, you should be at work, but instead of doing the job you were sent here for, you not only threaten to force the door of my laboratory, you question me as though I were a criminal suspect.'

His forehead was dripping with sweat. I controlled myself with an effort. I was determined to get through to him. I gritted my teeth and said:

'You *are* a suspect, Dr Sartorius. What is more, you're well aware of it!'

'Kelvin, unless you either retract or apologize, I shall lodge a complaint against you.'

'Why should I apologize? You're the one who barricaded himself in this laboratory instead of coming out to meet me, instead of telling me the truth about what is going on here. Have you gone completely mad? What are you – a scientist, or a miserable coward?'

I don't know what other insults I hurled at him. He did not even flinch. Globules of sweat trickled down over the enlarged pores of his cheeks. Suddenly I realized that he had not heard a word I was saying. Both hands behind his back, he was holding the door in position with all his strength; it was rattling as though someone inside were firing bursts from a machine-gun at the panel.

In a strange, high-pitched voice, he moaned:

'Go away. For God's sake, leave me. Go downstairs, I'll

join you later. I'll do whatever you want, only please go away now.'

His voice betrayed such exhaustion that instinctively I put out my arms to help him control the door. At this, he uttered a cry of horror, as though I had pointed a knife at him. As I retreated, he was shouting in his falsetto voice: 'Go away! Go away! I'm coming, I'm coming, I'm coming! No! No!' He opened the door and shot inside. I thought I saw a shining yellow disc flash across his chest.

Now a muffled clamour rose from the laboratory; a huge shadow appeared, as the curtain was brushed momentarily aside; then it fell back into place and I could see nothing more. What was happening inside that room? I heard running footsteps, as though a mad chase were in progress, followed by a terrifying crash of broken glass and the sound of a child's laugh.

My legs were trembling, and I stared at the door, appalled. The din had subsided, giving way to an uneasy silence. I sat down on a window ledge, too stunned to move; my head was splitting.

From where I was, I could see only a part of the corridor encircling the laboratory. I was at the summit of the Station, beneath the actual shell of the superstructure; the walls were concave and sloping, with oblong windows a few yards apart. The blue day was ending, and, as the shutters grated upwards, a blinding light shone through the thick glass. Every metal fitting, every latch and joint, blazed, and the great glass panel of the laboratory door glittered with pale coruscations. My hands looked grey in the spectral light. I noticed that I was holding the gas pistol; I had not realized that I had taken it out of its holster, and replaced it. What use could I have made of it – or even of a gamma pistol, had I had one? I could hardly have taken the laboratory by force.

I got up. The disc of the sun, reminiscent of a hydrogen explosion, was sinking into the ocean, and as I descended the stairway I was pierced by a jet of horizontal rays which was almost tangible. Halfway downstairs I paused to think, then went back up the steps and followed the corridor round the laboratory. Soon, I came across a second glass door, exactly like the first; I made no attempt to open it, knowing that it would be locked.

I was looking for an opening or vent of some sort. The idea of spying on Sartorius had come to me quite naturally, without the least sense of shame. I was determined to have done with conjecture and discover the truth, even if, as I imagined it would, the truth proved incomprehensible. It struck me that the laboratory must be lit from above by windows let into the dome. It should be possible, therefore, to spy on Sartorius from the outside. But first I should have to equip myself with an atmosphere suit and oxygen-gear.

When I reached the deck below, I found the door of the radio-cabin ajar. Snow, sunk in his armchair, was asleep. At the sound of my footsteps, he opened his eyes with a start.

'Hello, Kelvin!' he croaked. 'Well, did you discover anything?'

'Yes . . . he's not alone.'

Snow grinned sourly.

'Oh, really? Well, that's something. Has he got visitors?'

'I can't understand why you won't tell me what's going on,' I retorted impulsively. 'Since I have to remain here, I'm bound to find out the truth sooner or later. Why the mystery?'

'When you've received some visitors yourself, you'll understand.'

I had the impression that my presence annoyed him and he had no desire to prolong the conversation.

I turned to go.

'Where are you off to?'

I did not answer.

The hangar-deck was just as I had left it. My burnt-out capsule still stood there, gaping open, on its platform. On my way to select an atmosphere suit, I suddenly realized that

47

the skylights through which I hoped to observe Sartorius would probably be made of slabs of opaque glass, and I lost interest in my venture on to the outer hull.

Instead, I descended the spiral stairway which led to the lower-deck store-rooms. The cramped passage at the bottom contained the usual litter of crates and cylinders. The walls were sheeted in bare metal which had a bluish glint. A little further on, the frosted pipes of the refrigeration plant appeared beneath a vault and I followed them to the far end of the corridor where they vanished into a cooling-jacket with a wide, plastic collar. The door to the cold store was two inches thick and lagged with an insulating compound. When I opened it, the icy cold gripped me. I stood, shivering, on the threshold of a cave carved out of an iceberg; the huge coils, like sculptured reliefs, were hung with stalactites. Here, too, buried beneath a covering of snow, there were crates and cylinders, and shelves laden with boxes and transparent bags containing a yellow, oily substance. The vault sloped downwards to where a curtain of ice hid the back of the cave. I broke through it. An elongated figure, covered with a sheet of canvas, lay stretched out on an aluminium rack.

I lifted a corner of the canvas and recognized the stiff features of Gibarian. His glossy black hair clung tightly to his skull. The sinews of his throat stood out like bones. His glazed eyes stared up at the vault, a tear of opaque ice hanging from the corner of each lid. The cold was so intense that I had to clench my teeth to prevent them from chattering. I touched Gibarian's cheek; it was like touching a block of petrified wood, bristling with black prickly hairs. The curve of the lips seemed to express an infinite, disdainful patience.

As I let the canvas fall, I noticed, peeping out from beneath the folds at the foot, five round, shiny objects, like black pearls, ranged in order of size. I stiffened with horror.

What I had seen were the round pads of five bare toes. Under the shroud, flattened against Gibarian's body, lay the

Negress. Slowly, I pulled back the canvas. Her head, covered in frizzy hair twisted up into little tufts, was resting in the hollow of one massive arm. Her back glistened, the skin stretched taut over the spinal column. The huge body gave no sign of life. I looked again at the soles of her naked feet; they had not been flattened or deformed in any way by the weight which they had had to carry. Walking had not calloused the skin, which was as unblemished as that of her shoulders.

With a far greater effort than it had taken to touch Gibarian's corpse, I forced myself to touch one of the bare feet. Then I made a second bewildering discovery: this body, abandoned in a deep freeze, this apparent corpse, lived and moved. The woman had withdrawn her foot, like a sleeping dog when you try to take its paw.

She'll freeze, I thought confusedly, but her flesh had been warm to the touch, and I even imagined I had felt the regular beating of her pulse. I backed out and fled.

As I emerged from the white cave, the heat seemed suffocating. I climbed the spiral stairway back to the hangar-deck.

I sat on the hoops of a rolled-up parachute and put my head in my hands. I was stunned. My thoughts ran wild. What was happening to me? If my reason was giving way, the sooner I lost consciousness the better. The idea of sudden extinction aroused an inexpressible, unrealistic hope.

Useless to go and find Snow or Sartorius: no one could fully understand what I had just experienced, what I had seen, what I had touched with my own hands. There was only one possible explanation, one possible conclusion: madness. Yes, that was it, I had gone mad as soon as I arrived here. Emanations from the ocean had attacked my brain, and hallucination had followed hallucination. Rather than exhaust myself trying to solve these illusory riddles, I would do better to ask for medical assistance, to radio the *Prometheus* or some other vessel, to send out an SOS.

Then a curious change came over me: at the thought that I had gone mad, I calmed down.

And yet . . . I had heard Snow's words quite clearly. If, that is, Snow existed and I had ever spoken to him. The hallucinations might have begun much earlier. Perhaps I was still on board the *Prometheus*; perhaps I had been stricken with a sudden mental illness and was now confronting the creations of my own inflamed brain. Assuming that I was ill, there was reason to believe that I would get better, which gave me some hope of deliverance – a hope irreconcilable with a belief in the reality of the tangled nightmares through which I had just lived.

If only I could think up some experiment in logic – a key experiment – which would reveal whether I had really gone mad and was a helpless prey to the figments of my imagination, or whether, in spite of their ludicrous improbability, I had been experiencing real events.

As I turned all this over in my mind, I was looking at the monorail which led to the launching pad. It was a steel girder, painted pale green, a yard above the ground. Here and there, the paint was chipped, worn by the friction of the rocket trolleys. I touched the steel, feeling it grow warm beneath my fingers, and rapped the metal plating with my knuckles. Could madness attain such a degree of reality? Yes, I answered myself. After all, it was my own subject, I knew what I was talking about.

But was it possible to work out a controlled experiment? At first I told myself that it was not, since my sick brain (if it really was sick) would create the illusions I demanded of it. Even while dreaming, when we are in perfectly good health, we talk to strangers, put questions to them and hear their replies. Moreover, although our interlocutors are in fact the creations of our own psychic activity, evolved by a pseudo-independent process, until they have spoken to us we do not know what words will emerge from their lips. And yet these words have been formulated by a separate part of our own minds; we should therefore be aware of them at the very moment that we think them up in order to put them into the mouths of imaginary beings. Consequently, whatever form my proposed test were to take, and whatever method I used to put it into execution, there was always the possibility that I was behaving exactly as in a dream. Neither Snow nor Sartorius having any real existence, it would be pointless to put questions to them.

I thought of taking some powerful drug, peyotl for example, or another preparation inducing vivid hallucinations. If visions ensued, this would prove that I had really experienced these recent events and that they were part and parcel of the surrounding material reality. But then, no, I thought, this would not constitute the proof I needed, since I knew the effects of the drug (which I should have chosen for myself) and my imagination could suggest to me the double illusion of having taken the drug and of experiencing its effects.

I was going around in circles; there seemed to be no escape. It was not possible to think except with one's brain, no one could stand outside himself in order to check the functioning of his inner processes. Suddenly an idea struck me, as simple as it was effective.

I leapt to my feet and ran to the radio-cabin. The room was deserted. I glanced at the electric clock on the wall. Nearly four o'clock, the fourth hour of the Station's artificial night-time. Outside, the red sun was shining. I quickly plugged in the long-range transmitter, and while the valves warmed up, I went over in my mind the principal stages of the experiment.

I could not remember the call-sign for the automatic station on the satellite, but I found it on a card hanging above the main instrument panel, sent it out in Morse, and received the answering signal eight seconds later. The satellite, or rather its electronic brain, identified itself by a rhythmic pulse.

I instructed the satellite to give me the figures for the galactic meridians it was traversing at twenty-two-second intervals while orbiting Solaris, and I specified an answer to five decimal points.

Then I sat and waited for the reply. Ten minutes later, it arrived. I tore off the strip of freshly printed paper and hid it in a drawer, taking care not to look at it. I went to the bookcase and took out the big galactic charts, the logarithm tables, a calendar giving the daily path of the satellite, and various other textbooks. Then I sat down to work out for myself the answer to the question I had posed. For an hour or more, I integrated the equations. It was a long time since I had tackled such elaborate calculations. My last major effort in this direction must have been my practical astronomy exam.

I worked at the problem with the help of the Station's giant computer. My reasoning went as follows: by making my calculations from the galactic charts, I would obtain an approximate cross-check with the results provided by the satellite. Approximate because the path of the satellite was subject to very complex variations due to the effects of the gravitational forces of Solaris and its two suns, as well as to the local variations in gravity caused by the ocean. When I had the two series of figures, one furnished by the satellite and the other calculated theoretically on the basis of the galactic charts, I would make the necessary adjustments and the two groups would then coincide up to the fourth decimal point, discrepancies due to the unforeseeable influence of the ocean arising only at the fifth.

If the figures obtained from the satellite were simply the product of my deranged mind, they could not possibly coincide with the second series. My brain might be unhinged, but it could not conceivably compete with the Station's giant computer and secretly perform calculations requiring several months' work. Therefore, if the figures corresponded, it would follow that the Station's computer really existed, that I had really used it, and that I was not delirious.

My hands trembled as I took the telegraphic tape out of the drawer and laid it alongside the wide band of paper from the computer. As I had predicted, the two series of numbers corresponded up to the fourth decimal point.

I put all the papers away in the drawer. So the computer existed independently of me; that meant that the Station and its inhabitants really existed too.

As I was closing the drawer, I noticed that it was stuffed with sheets of paper covered with hastily scribbled sums. A single glance told me that someone had already attempted an experiment similar to mine and had asked the satellite, not for information about the galactic meridians, but for the measurements of Solaris's albedo at intervals of forty seconds.

I was not mad. The last ray of hope was extinguished. I unplugged the transmitter, drank the remains of the soup in the vacuum flask, and went to bed.

Rheya

Desperation and a sort of dumb rage had sustained me while working with the computer. Now, overcome with exhaustion, I could not even remember how to let down a mechanical bed. Forgetting to push back the clamps, I hung on to the handle with all my weight and the mattress tumbled down on top of me.

I tore off my clothes and flung them away from me, then collapsed on to the pillow, without even taking the trouble to inflate it properly. I fell asleep with the lights on.

I reopened my eyes with the impression of having dozed off for only a few minutes. The room was bathed in a dim red light. It was cooler, and I felt refreshed.

I lay there, the bedclothes pushed back, completely naked. The curtains were half drawn, and there, opposite me, beside the window-pane lit by the red sun, someone was sitting. It was Rheya. She was wearing a white beach dress, the material stretched tightly over her breasts. She sat with her legs crossed; her feet were bare. Motionless, leaning on her sun-tanned arms, she gazed at me from beneath her black lashes: Rheya, with her dark hair brushed back. For a long time, I lay there peacefully gazing back at her. My first thought was reassuring: I was dreaming and I was aware that I was dreaming. Nevertheless, I would have preferred her not to be there. I closed my eyes and tried to shake off the dream. When I opened them again, Rheya was still sitting opposite me. Her lips were pouting slightly – a habit of hers – as though she were about to whistle; but her expression was serious. I thought of my recent speculations on the subject of dreams.

She had not changed since the day I had seen her for the

last time; she was then a girl of nineteen. Today, she would be twenty-nine. But, evidently, the dead do not change; they remain eternally young. She went on gazing at me, an expression of surprise on her face. I thought of throwing something at her, but, even in a dream, I could not bring myself to harm a dead person.

I murmured: 'Poor little thing, have you come to visit me?'

The sound of my voice frightened me; the room, Rheya, everything seemed extraordinarily real. A three-dimensional dream, coloured in half-tones . . . I saw several objects on the floor which I had not noticed when I went to bed. When I wake up, I told myself, I shall check whether these things are still there or whether, like Rheya, I only saw them in a dream.

'Do you mean to stay for long?' I asked. I realized that I was speaking very softly, like someone afraid of being over-heard. Why worry about eavesdroppers in a dream?

The sun was rising over the horizon. A good sign. I had gone to bed during a red day, which should have been suc-ceeded by a blue day, followed by another red day. I had not slept for fifteen hours at a stretch. So it *was* dream!

Reassured, I looked closely at Rheya. She was silhouetted against the sun. The scarlet rays cast a glow over the smooth skin of her left cheek and the shadows of her eyelashes fell across her face. How pretty she was! Even in my sleep my memory of her was uncannily precise. I watched the move-ments of the sun, waiting to see the dimple appear in that unusual place slightly below the corner of the lips. All the same, I would have preferred to wake up. It was time I did some work. I closed my eyelids tightly.

I heard a metallic noise, and opened my eyes again. Rheya was sitting beside me on the bed, still looking at me gravely. I smiled at her. She smiled back at me and leant forward. We kissed. First a timid, childish kiss, then more prolonged ones. I held her for a long time. Was it possible to feel so much in a dream, I wondered. I was not betraying her memory, for it

55

was of her that I was dreaming, only her. It had never happened to me before . . .

Was it then that I began to have doubts? I went on telling myself that it was a dream, but my heart tightened.

I tensed my muscles, ready to leap out of bed. I was half-expecting to fail, for often, in dreams, your sluggish body refuses to respond. I hoped that the effort would drag me out of sleep. But I did not wake; I sat on the edge of the bed, my legs dangling. There was nothing for it, I should have to endure this dream right to the bitter end. My feeling of well-being had vanished. I was afraid.

'What . . .' I asked. I cleared my throat. 'What do you want?'

I felt around the floor with my bare feet, searching for a pair of slippers. I stubbed my toe against a sharp edge, and stifled a cry of pain. That'll wake me up, I thought with satisfaction, at the same time remembering that I had no slippers.

But still it went on. Rheya had drawn back and was leaning against the end of the bed. Her dress rose and fell lightly with her breathing. She watched me with quiet interest.

Quick, I thought, a shower! But then I realized that in a dream a shower would not interrupt my sleep.

'Where have you come from?'

She seized my hand and, with a gesture I knew well, threw it up and caught it again, then played with my fingers.

'I don't know,' she replied. 'Are you angry?'

It was her voice, that familiar, low-pitched, slightly far-away voice, and that air of not caring much about what she was saying, of already being preoccupied with something else. People used to think her off-hand, even rude, because the expression on her face rarely changed from one of vague astonishment.

'Did . . . did anyone see you?'

'I don't know. I got here without any trouble. Why, Kris, is it important?'

She was still playing with my fingers, but her face now wore a slight frown.

'Rheya.'

'What, my darling?'

'How did you know where I was?'

She pondered. A broad smile revealed her teeth.

'I haven't the faintest idea. Isn't it funny? When I came in you were asleep. I didn't wake you up because you get cross so easily. You have a very bad temper.'

She squeezed my hand.

'Did you go down below?'

'Yes. It was all frozen. I ran away.'

She let go of my hand and lay back. With her hair falling to one side, she looked at me with the half-smile that had irritated me before it had captivated me.

'But, Rheya . . .' I stammered.

I leant over her and turned back the short sleeve of her dress. There, just above her vaccination scar, was a red dot, the mark of a hypodermic needle. I was not really surprised, but my heart gave a lurch.

I touched the red spot with my finger. For years now I had dreamt of it, over and over again, always waking with a shudder to find myself in the same position, doubled up between the crumpled sheets – just as I had found *her*, already growing cold. It was as though, in my sleep, I tried to relive what she had gone through; as though I hoped to turn back the clock and ask her forgiveness, or keep her company during those final minutes when she was feeling the effects of the injection and was overcome by terror. She, who dreaded the least scratch, who hated pain or the sight of blood, had deliberately done this horrible thing, leaving nothing but a few scribbled words addressed to me. I had kept her note in my wallet. By now it was soiled and creased, but I had never had the heart to throw it away.

Time and time again I had imagined her tracing those words and making her final preparations. I persuaded myself that she had only been play-acting, that she had wanted to frighten me and had taken an overdose by mistake. Everyone told me that it must have happened like that, or else it had been a spontaneous decision, the result of a sudden depression. But people knew nothing of what I had said to her five days earlier; they did not know that, in order to twist the knife more cruelly, I had taken away my belongings and that she, as I was closing my suitcases, had said, very calmly: 'I suppose you know what this means?' And I had pretended not to understand, even though I knew quite well what she meant; I thought her too much of a coward, and had even told her as much . . . And now she was lying across the bed, looking at me attentively, as though she did not know that it was I who had killed her.

'Well?' she asked. Her eyes reflected the red sun. The entire room was red. Rheya looked at her arm with interest, because I had been examining it for so long, and when I drew back she laid her smooth, cool cheek in the palm of my hand.

'Rheya,' I stammered, 'it's not possible . . .'

'Hush!'

I could sense the movement of her eyes beneath their closed lids.

'Where are we, Rheya?'

'At home.'

'Where's that?'

One eye opened and shut again instantly. The long lashes tickled my palm.

'Kris.'

'What?'

'I'm happy.'

Raising my head, I could see part of the bed in the washbasin mirror: a cascade of soft hair – Rheya's hair – and my bare knees. I pulled towards me with my foot one of the misshapen objects I had found in the box and picked it up with my free hand. It was a spindle, one end of which had melted to a needle-point. I held the point to my skin and dug it in, just beside a small pink scar. The pain shot through my whole body. I watched the blood run down the inside of my thigh and drip noiselessly on to the floor.

What was the use? Terrifying thoughts assailed me, thoughts which were taking a definite shape. I no longer told myself: It's a dream. I had ceased to believe that. Now I was thinking: I must be ready to defend myself.

I examined her shoulders, her hip under the close-fitting white dress, and her dangling naked feet. Leaning forward, I took hold of one of her ankles and ran my fingers over the sole of her foot.

The skin was soft, like that of a newborn child.

I knew then that it was not Rheya, and I was almost certain that she herself did not know it.

The bare foot wriggled and Rheya's lips parted in silent laughter.

'Stop it,' she murmured.

Cautiously I withdrew my hand from under the cheek and stood up. Then I dressed quickly. She sat up and watched me.

'Where are your things?' I asked her. Immediately, I regretted my question.

'My things?'

'Don't you have anything except that dress?'

From now on, I would pursue the game with my eyes open. I tried to appear unconcerned, indifferent, as though we had parted only yesterday, as though we had never parted.

She stood up. With a familiar gesture, she tugged at her skirt to smooth out the creases. My words had worried her, but she said nothing. For the first time, she examined the room with an enquiring, scrutinizing gaze. Then, puzzled, she replied:

'I don't know.' She opened the locker door. 'In here, perhaps?'

'No, there's nothing but work-suits in there.'

I found an electric point by the basin and began to shave, careful not to take my eyes off her.

She went to and fro, rummaging everywhere. Eventually, she came up to me and said:

'Kris, I have the feeling that something's happened . . .'

She broke off. I unplugged the razor, and waited.

'I have the feeling that I've forgotten something,' she went on, 'that I've forgotten a lot of things. I can only remember you. I . . . I can't remember anything else.'

I listened to her, forcing myself to look unconcerned.

'Have I . . . Have I been ill?' she asked.

'Yes . . . in a way. Yes, you've been slightly ill.'

'There you are then. That explains my lapses of memory.'

She had brightened up again. Never shall I be able to describe how I felt then. As I watched her moving about the room, now smiling, now serious, talkative one moment, silent the next, sitting down and then getting up again, my terror was gradually overcome by the conviction that it was the real Rheya there in the room with me, even though my reason told me that she seemed somehow stylized, reduced to certain characteristic expressions, gestures and movements.

Suddenly, she clung to me.

'What's happening to us, Kris?' She pressed her fists against my chest. 'Is everything all right? Is there something wrong?'

'Things couldn't be better.'

She smiled wanly.

'When you answer me like that, it means things could hardly be worse.'

'What nonsense!' I said hurriedly. 'Rheya, my darling, I must leave you. Wait here for me.' And, because I was becoming extremely hungry, I added: 'Would you like something to eat?'

'To eat?' She shook her head. 'No. Will I have to wait long for you?'

'Only an hour.'

'I'm coming with you.'

'You can't come with me. I've got work to do.'

'I'm coming with you.'

She had changed. This was not Rheya at all; the real Rheya never imposed herself, would never have forced her presence on me.

'It's impossible, my sweet.'

She looked me up and down. Then suddenly she seized my hand. And my hand lingered, moved up her warm, rounded arm. In spite of myself I was caressing her. My body recognized her body; my body desired her, my body was attracted towards hers beyond reason, beyond thought, beyond fear.

Desperately trying to remain calm, I repeated:

'Rheya, it's out of the question. You must stay here.'

A single word echoed round the room:

'No.'

'Why?'

'I . . . I don't know.' She looked around her, then, once more, raised her eyes to mine. 'I can't,' she whispered.

'But why?'

'I don't know. I can't. It's as though . . . as though . . .' She searched for the answer which, as she uttered it, seemed to come to her like a revelation. 'It's as though I mustn't let you out of my sight.'

The resolute tone of her voice scarcely suggested an avowal of affection; it implied something quite different. With this realization, the manner in which I was embracing Rheya underwent an abrupt, though not immediately noticeable, change.

I was holding her in my arms and gazing into her eyes.

Imperceptibly, almost instinctively, I began to pull her hands together behind her back at the same time searching the room with my eyes: I needed something with which to tie her hands.

Suddenly she jerked her elbows together, and there followed a powerful recoil. I resisted for barely a second. Thrown backwards and almost lifted off my feet, even had I been an athlete I could not have freed myself. Rheya straightened up and dropped her arms to her sides. Her face, lit by an uncertain smile, had played no part in the struggle.

She was gazing at me with the same calm interest as when I had first awakened – as though she was utterly unmoved by my desperate ploy, as though she was quite unaware that anything had happened, and had not noticed my sudden panic. She stood before me, waiting – grave, passive, mildly surprised.

Leaving Rheya in the middle of the room, I went over to the washbasin. I was a prisoner, caught in an absurd trap from which at all costs I was determined to escape. I would have been incapable of putting into words the meaning of what had happened or what was going through my mind; but now I realized that my situation was identical with that of the other inhabitants of the Station, that everything I had experienced, discovered or guessed at was part of a single whole, terrifying and incomprehensible. Meanwhile, I was racking my brain to think up some ruse, to work out some means of escape. Without turning round, I could feel Rheya's eyes following me. There was a medicine chest above the basin. Quickly I went through its contents, and found a bottle of sleeping pills. I shook out four tablets – the maximum dose – into a glass, and filled it with hot water. I made little effort to conceal my actions from Rheya. Why? I did not even bother to ask myself.

When the tablets had dissolved, I returned to Rheya, who was still standing in the same place.

'Are you angry with me?' she asked, in a low voice.

'No. Drink this.'

Unconsciously, I had known all along that she would obey me. She took the glass without a word and drank the scalding mixture in one gulp. Putting down the empty glass on a stool, I went and sat in a chair in the corner of the room.

Rheya joined me, squatting on the floor in her accustomed manner with her legs folded under her, and tossing back her hair. I was no longer under any illusion: this was not Rheya – and yet I recognized her every habitual gesture. Horror gripped me by the throat; and what was most horrible was that I must go on tricking her, pretending to take her for Rheya, while she herself sincerely believed that she *was* Rheya – of that I was certain, if one could be certain of anything any longer.

She was leaning against my knees, her hair brushing my hand. We remained thus for some while. From time to time, I glanced at my watch. Half an hour went by; the sleeping tablets should have started to work. Rheya murmured something.

'What did you say?'

There was no reply.

Although I attributed her silence to the onset of sleep, secretly I doubted the effectiveness of the pills. Once again, I did not ask myself why. Perhaps it was because my subterfuge seemed too simple.

Slowly her head slid across my knees, her dark hair falling over her face. Her breathing grew deeper and more regular; she was asleep. I stooped in order to lift her on to the bed. As I did so, her eyes opened; she put her arms round my neck and burst into shrill laughter.

I was dumbfounded. Rheya could hardly contain her mirth. With an expression that was at once ingenuous and sly, she observed me through half-closed eyelids. I sat down again, tense, stupefied, at a loss. With a final burst of laughter, she snuggled against my legs.

In an expressionless voice, I asked:

'Why are you laughing?'

Once again, a look of anxiety and surprise came over her face. It was clear that she wanted to give me an honest explanation. She sighed, and rubbed her nose like a child.

'I don't know,' she said at last, with genuine puzzlement. 'I'm behaving like an idiot, aren't I? But so are you . . . you look idiotic, all stiff and pompous like . . . like Pelvis.'

I could hardly believe my ears.

'Like who?'

'Like Pelvis. You know who I mean, that fat man. . . .'

Rheya could not possibly have known Pelvis, or even heard me mention him, for the simple reason that he had returned from an expedition three years after her death. I had not known him previously and was therefore unaware of his inveterate habit, when presiding over meetings at the Institute, of letting sessions drag on indefinitely. Moreover, his name was Pelle Villis and until his return I did not know that he had been nicknamed Pelvis.

Rheya leant her elbows on my knees and looked me in the eyes. I put out my hand and stroked her arms, her shoulders and the base of her bare neck, which pulsed beneath my fingers. While it looked as though I was caressing her (and indeed, judging by her expression, that was how she interpreted the touch of my hands) in reality I was verifying once again that her body was warm to the touch, an ordinary human body, with muscles, bones, joints. Gazing calmly into her eyes, I felt a hideous desire to tighten my grip.

Suddenly I remembered Snow's bloodstained hands, and let go.

'How you stare at me,' Rheya said, placidly.

My heart was beating so furiously that I was incapable of speech. I closed my eyes. In that very instant, complete in every detail, a plan of action sprang to my mind. There was not a second to lose. I stood up.

'I must go out, Rheya. If you absolutely insist on coming with me, I'll take you.'

'Good.'

She jumped to her feet.

I opened the locker and selected a suit for each of us. Then I asked:

'Why are you barefoot?'

She answered hesitantly:

'I don't know . . . I must have left my shoes somewhere.'

I did not pursue the matter.

'You'll have to take your dress off to put this on.'

'Flying-overalls? What for?'

As she tried to take off her dress, an extraordinary fact became apparent: there were no zips, or fastenings of any sort; the red buttons down the front were merely decorative. Rheya smiled, embarrassed.

As though it were the most normal way of going about it, I picked up some kind of scalpel from the floor and slit the dress down the back from neck to waist, so that she could pull it over her head.

When she had put on the flying-overalls (which were slightly too large for her) and we were about to leave, she asked:

'Are we going on a flight?'

I merely nodded. I was afraid of running into Snow. But the dome was empty and the door leading to the radio-cabin was shut.

A deathly silence still hung over the hangar-deck. Rheya followed my movements attentively. I opened a stall and examined the shuttle vehicle inside. I checked, one after another, the micro-reactor, the controls and the diffusers. Then, having removed the empty capsule from its stand, I aimed the electric trolley towards the sloping runway.

I had chosen a small shuttle used for ferrying stores between the Station and the satellite, one that did not nor-mally carry personnel since it did not open from the inside. The choice was carefully calculated in accordance with my plan. Of course, I had no intention of launching it, but I simulated the preparations for an actual departure. Rheya, who had so often accompanied me on my space-flights, was familiar with the preliminary routine. Inside the cockpit, I checked that the climatization and oxygen-supply systems were functioning. I switched on the main circuit and the indicators on the instrument panel lit up. I climbed out and said to Rheya, who was waiting at the foot of the ladder:

'Get in.'

'What about you?'

'I'll follow you. I have to close the hatch behind us.'

She gave no sign that she suspected any trickery. When she had disappeared inside, I stuck my head into the opening and asked:

'Are you comfortable?'

I heard a muffled 'yes' from inside the confined cockpit. I withdrew my head and slammed the hatch to with all my strength. I slid home the two bolts and tightened the five safety screws with the special spanner I had brought with me. The slender metal cigar stood there, pointing upwards, as though it were really about to take off into space.

Its captive was in no danger: the oxygen-tanks were full and there were food supplies in the cockpit. In any case, I did not intend to keep her prisoner indefinitely. I desperately needed two hours of freedom in order to concentrate on the decisions which had to be taken and to work out a joint plan of action with Snow.

As I was tightening the last screw but one, I felt a vibration in the three-pronged clamp which held the base of the shuttle. I thought I must have loosened the support in my over-eager handling of the heavy spanner, but when I stepped back to take a look, I was greeted by a spectacle which I hope I shall never have to see again.

The whole vehicle trembled, shaken from the inside as though by some superhuman force. Not even a steel robot could have imparted such a convulsive tremor to an eight-ton mass, and yet the cabin contained only a frail, dark-haired girl.

The reflections from the lights quivered on the shuttle's gleaming sides. I could not hear the blows; there was no sound whatever from inside the vehicle. But the outspread struts vibrated like taut wires. The violence of the shock-waves was such that I was afraid the entire scaffolding would collapse.

I tightened the final screw with a trembling hand, threw down the spanner and jumped off the ladder. As I slowly retreated, I noticed that the shock-absorbers, designed to resist a continuous pressure, were vibrating furiously. It looked to me as though the shuttle's outer skin was wrinkling.

Frenziedly, I rushed to the control-panel and with both hands lifted the starting lever. As I did so the intercom connected to the shuttle's interior gave out a piercing sound – not a cry, but a sound which bore not the slightest resemblance to the human voice, in which I could nevertheless just make out my name, repeated over and over again: 'Kris! Kris! Kris!'

I had attacked the controls so violently, fumbling in my haste, that my fingers were torn and bleeding.

A bluish glimmer, like that of a ghostly dawn, lit up the walls. Swirling clouds of vaporous dust eddied round the launching pad; the dust turned into a column of fierce sparks and the echoes of a thunderous roar drowned all other noise. Three flames, merging instantly into a single pillar of fire, lifted the craft, which rose up through the open hatch in the dome, leaving behind a glowing trail which rippled as it gradually subsided. Shutters slid over the hatch, and the automatic ventilators began to suck in the acrid smoke which billowed round the room.

It was only later that I remembered all these details; at the time, I hardly knew what I was seeing. Clinging to the control-panel, the fierce heat burning my face and singeing my hair, I gulped the acrid air which smelt of a mixture of burning fuel and the ozone given off by ionization. I had instinctively closed my eyes at the moment of lift-off, but the glare had penetrated my eyelids. For some time, I saw nothing but black, red and gold spirals which slowly died away. The ventilators continued to hum; the smoke and the dust were gradually clearing.

The green glow of the radar-screen caught my eye. My hands flew across its controls as I began to search for the shuttle. By the time I had located it, it was already flying above the atmosphere. I had never launched a vehicle in such a blind and unthinking way, with no pre-set speed or direction. I did not even know its range and was afraid of causing some unpredictable disaster. I judged that the easiest thing to do would be to place it in a stationary orbit around Solaris and then cut the engines. I verified from the tables that the required altitude was 725 miles. It was no guarantee, of course, but I could see no other way out.

I did not have the heart to switch on the intercom, which had been disconnected at lift-off. I could not bear to expose myself again to the sound of that horrifying voice, which was no longer even remotely human.

I felt I was justified in thinking that I had defeated the 'simulacra', and that behind the illusion, contrary to all expectation, I had found the real Rheya again – the Rheya of my memories, whom the hypothesis of madness would have destroyed.

At one o'clock, I left the hangar-deck.

The Little Apocrypha

My face and hands were badly burnt. I remembered noticing a jar of anti-burn ointment when I was looking for sleeping pills for Rheya (I was in no mood to laugh at my naïveté), so I went back to my room.

I opened the door. The room was glowing in the red twilight. Someone was sitting in the armchair where Rheya had knelt. For a second or two, I was paralysed with terror, filled with an overwhelming desire to turn and run. Then the seated figure raised its head: it was Snow. His legs crossed, still wearing the acid-stained trousers, he was looking through some papers, a pile of which lay on a small table beside him. He put down those he was holding in his hand, let his glasses slide down his nose, and scowled up at me.

Without saying a word, I went to the basin, took the ointment out of the medicine chest and applied it to my forehead and cheeks. Fortunately my face was not too swollen and my eyes, which I had closed instinctively, did not seem to be inflamed. I lanced some large blisters on my temples and cheekbones with a sterilized needle; they exuded a serous liquid, which I mopped up with an antiseptic pad. Then I applied some gauze dressing.

Snow watched me throughout these first-aid operations, but I paid no attention to him. When at last I had finished (and my burns had become even more painful), I sat myself down in the other chair. I had first to remove Rheya's dress – that apparently quite normal dress which was nevertheless devoid of fastenings.

Snow, his hands clasped around one bony knee, continued to observe me with a critical air.

69

'Well, are you ready to have a chat?' he asked.

I did not answer; I was busy replacing a piece of gauze which had slipped down one cheek.

'You've had a visitor, haven't you?'

'Yes,' I answered curtly.

He had begun the conversation on a note which I found displeasing.

'And you've rid yourself of it already? Well, well! That was quick!'

He touched his forehead, which was still peeling and mottled with pink patches of new skin. I was thunderstruck. Why had I not realized before the implications of Snow's and Sartorius's 'sunburn'? No one exposed himself to the sun here.

Without noticing my sudden change of expression he went on:

'I imagine you didn't try extreme methods straight away. What did you use first – drugs, poison, judo?'

'Do you want to discuss the thing seriously or play the fool? If you don't want to help, you can leave me in peace.'

He half-closed his eyes.

'Sometimes one plays the fool in spite of oneself. Did you try the rope, or the hammer? Or the well-aimed ink-bottle, like Luther? No?' He grimaced. 'Aren't you a fast worker! The basin is still intact, you haven't banged your head against the walls, you haven't even turned the room upside down. One, two and into the rocket, just like that!' He looked at his watch. 'Consequently, we have two or three hours at our disposal . . . Am I getting on your nerves?' he added, with a disagreeable smile.

'Yes,' I said curtly.

'Really? Well, if I tell you a little story, will you believe me?'

I said nothing.

Still with that hideous smile, he went on:

70

'It started with Gibarian. He locked himself in his cabin and refused to talk to us except through the door. And can you guess what we thought?'

I remained silent.

'Naturally, we thought he had gone mad. He let a bit of it out – through the locked door – but not everything. You may wonder why he didn't tell us that there was someone with him. Oh, *suum cuique*! But he was a true scientist. He begged us to let him take his chance!'

'What chance?'

'He was obviously doing his damnedest to solve the problem, to get to the bottom of it. He worked day and night. You know what he was doing? You must know.'

'Those calculations, in the drawer of the radio-cabin – were they his?'

'Yes.'

'How long did it go on?'

'This visit? About a week . . . We thought he was suffering from hallucinations, or having a nervous breakdown. I gave him some scopolamine.'

'Gave him?'

'Yes. He took it, but not for himself. He tried it out on someone else.'

'What did you do?'

'On the third day we had decided, if all else failed, to break down the door, maybe injuring his self-esteem, but at least curing him.'

'Ah . . .'

'Yes.'

'So, in that locker . . .'

'Yes, my friend, quite. But in the meantime, we too had received visitors. We had our hands full, and didn't have a chance to tell him what was going on. Now it's . . . it's become a routine.'

He spoke so softly that I guessed rather than heard the last few words.

'I still don't understand!' I exclaimed. 'If you listened at his door, you must have heard two voices.'

'No, we heard only his voice. There were strange noises, but we thought they came from him too.'

'Only his voice! But how is it that you didn't hear . . . her?'

'I don't know. I have the rudiments of a theory about it, but I've dropped it for the moment. No point getting bogged down in details. But what about you? You must already have seen something yesterday, otherwise you would have taken us for lunatics.'

'I thought it was I who had gone mad.'

'So you didn't see anyone?'

'I saw someone.'

'Who?'

I gave him a long look – he no longer wore even the semblance of a smile – and answered:

'That . . . that black woman . . .' He was leaning forward, and as I spoke his body almost imperceptibly relaxed. 'You might have warned me.'

'I did warn you.

'You could have chosen a better way!'

'It was the only way possible. I didn't know what you would see. No one could know, no one ever knows . . .'

'Listen, Snow, I want to ask you something. You've had some experience of this . . . phenomenon. Will she . . . will the person who visited me today . . .?'

'Will she come back, do you mean?'

I nodded.

'Yes and no,' he said.

'What does that mean?'

'She . . . this person will come back as though nothing had happened, just as she was at the beginning of her first visit. More precisely, she will appear not to realize what you did to get rid of her. If you abide by the rules, she won't be aggressive.'

'What rules?'

'That depends on the circumstances.'

'Snow!'

'What?'

'Don't let's waste time talking in riddles.'

'In riddles? Kelvin, I'm afraid you still don't understand.'
His eyes glittered. 'All right, then!' he went on, brutally. 'Can
you tell me who your visitor was?'

I swallowed my saliva and turned away. I did not want to
look at him. I would have preferred to be dealing with anyone else but him; but I had no choice. A piece of gauze came
unstuck and fell on my hand. I gave a start.

'A woman who . . .' I stopped. 'She died. An injection . . .'

'Suicide?'

'Yes.'

'Is that all?' He waited. Seeing that I remained silent, he
murmured: 'No, it's not all . . .'

I looked up quickly; he was not looking at me.

'How did you guess?' He said nothing. 'It's true, there's
more to it than that.' I moistened my lips. 'We quarrelled. Or
rather, I lost my temper and said a lot of things I didn't mean.
I packed my bags and cleared out. She had given me to
understand . . . not in so many words – when one's lived
together for years it's not necessary. I was certain she didn't
mean it, that she wouldn't dare, she'd be too afraid, and I
told her so. Next day, I remembered I'd left these . . . these
ampoules in a drawer. She knew they were there. I'd brought
them back from the laboratory because I needed them, and I
had explained to her that the effect of a heavy dose would be
lethal. I was a bit worried. I wanted to go back and get them,
but I thought that would give the impression that I'd taken
her remarks seriously. By the third day I was really worried
and made up my mind to go back. When I arrived, she was
dead.'

'You poor innocent!'

I looked up with a start. But Snow was not making fun of
me. It seemed to me that I was seeing him now for the first

time. His face was grey, and the deep lines between cheek and nose were evidence of an unutterable exhaustion: he looked a sick man.

Curiously awed, I asked him:

'Why did you say that?'

'Because it's a tragic story.' Seeing that I was upset, he added, hastily: 'No, no, you still don't understand. Of course it's a terrible burden to carry around, and you must feel like a murderer, but . . . there are worse things.'

'Oh, really?'

'Yes, really. And I'm almost glad that you refuse to believe me. Certain events, which have actually happened, are horrible, but what is more horrible still is what hasn't happened, what has never existed.'

'What are you saying?' I asked, my voice faltering.

He shook his head from side to side.

'A normal man,' he said. 'What is a normal man? A man who has never committed a disgraceful act? Maybe, but has he never had uncontrollable thoughts? Perhaps he hasn't. But perhaps something, a phantasm, rose up from somewhere within him, ten or thirty years ago, something which he suppressed and then forgot about, which he doesn't fear since he knows he will never allow it to develop and so lead to any action on his part. And now, suddenly, in broad daylight, he comes across this thing . . . this thought, embodied, riveted to him, indestructible. He wonders where he is . . . Do you know where he is?'

'Where?'

'Here,' whispered Snow, 'on Solaris.'

'But what does it mean? After all, you and Sartorius aren't criminals . . .'

'And you call yourself a psychologist, Kelvin! Who hasn't had, at some moment in his life, a crazy daydream, an obsession? Imagine . . . imagine a fetishist who becomes infatuated with, let's say, a grubby piece of cloth, and who threatens and entreats and defies every risk in order to

74

acquire this beloved bit of rag. A peculiar idea, isn't it? A man who at one and the same time is ashamed of the object of his desire and cherishes it above everything else, a man who is ready to sacrifice his life for his love, since the feeling he has for it is perhaps as overwhelming as Romeo's feeling for Juliet. Such cases exist, as you know. So, in the same way, there are things, situations, that no one has dared to externalize, but which the mind has produced by accident in a moment of aberration, of madness, call it what you will. At the next stage, the idea becomes flesh and blood. That's all.'

Stupefied, my mouth dry, I repeated:

'That's all?' My head was spinning. 'And what about the Station? What has it got to do with the Station?'

'It's almost as if you're purposely refusing to understand,' he groaned. 'I've been talking about Solaris the whole time, solely about Solaris. If the truth is hard to swallow, it's not my fault. Anyhow, after what you've already been through, you ought to be able to hear me out! We take off into the cosmos, ready for anything: for solitude, for hardship, for exhaustion, death. Modesty forbids us to say so, but there are times when we think pretty well of ourselves. And yet, if we examine it more closely, our enthusiasm turns out to be all sham. We don't want to conquer the cosmos, we simply want to extend the boundaries of Earth to the frontiers of the cosmos. For us, such and such a planet is as arid as the Sahara, another as frozen as the North Pole, yet another as lush as the Amazon basin. We are humanitarian and chivalrous; we don't want to enslave other races, we simply want to bequeath them our values and take over their heritage in exchange. We think of ourselves as the Knights of the Holy Contact. This is another lie. We are only seeking Man. We have no need of other worlds. We need mirrors. We don't know what to do with other worlds. A single world, our own, suffices us; but we can't accept it for what it is. We are searching for an ideal image of our own world: we go in quest of a planet, of a civilization superior to our own but

75

developed on the basis of a prototype of our primeval past. At the same time, there is something inside us which we don't like to face up to, from which we try to protect ourselves, but which nevertheless remains, since we don't leave Earth in a state of primal innocence. We arrive here as we are in reality, and when the page is turned and that reality is revealed to us – that part of our reality which we would prefer to pass over in silence – then we don't like it any more.'

I had listened to him patiently.

'But what on earth are you talking about?'

'I'm talking about what we all wanted: contact with another civilization. Now we've got it! And we can observe, through a microscope, as it were, our own monstrous ugliness, our folly, our shame!' His voice shook with rage.

'So ... you think it's ... the ocean? That the ocean is responsible for it all? But why? I'm not asking how, I'm simply asking why? Do you seriously think that it wants to toy with us, or punish us – a sort of elementary demonomania? A planet dominated by a huge devil, who satisfies the demands of his satanic humour by sending succubi to haunt the members of a scientific expedition ...? Snow, you can't believe anything so absurd!'

He muttered under his breath.

'This devil isn't such a fool as all that ...'

I looked at him in amazement. Perhaps what had happened, assuming that we had experienced it in our right minds, had finally driven him over the edge? A reaction psychosis?

He was laughing to himself.

'Making your diagnosis? Don't be in too much of a hurry! You've only been through one ordeal – and that a reasonably mild one.'

'Oh, so the devil had pity on me!'

I was beginning to weary of this conversation.

'What is it you want exactly?' Snow went on. 'Do you want me to tell you what this mass of metamorphic plasma *x*-billion tons of metamorphic plasma – is scheming against us? Perhaps nothing.'

'What do you mean, nothing?'

Snow smiled.

'You must know that science is concerned with phenomena rather than causes. The phenomena here began to manifest themselves eight or nine days after that X-ray experiment. Perhaps the ocean reacted to the irradiation with a counter-irradiation, perhaps it probed our brains and penetrated to some kind of psychic tumour.'

I pricked up my ears.

'Tumour?'

'Yes, isolated psychic processes, enclosed, stifled, encysted – foci smouldering under the ashes of memory. It deciphered them and made use of them, in the same way as one uses a recipe or a blueprint. You know how alike the asymmetric crystalline structures of a chromosome are to those of the DNA molecule, one of the constituents of the cerebrosides which constitute the substratum of the memory-processes? This genetic substance is a plasma which "remembers". The ocean has "read" us by this means, registering the minutest details, with the result that . . . well, you know the result. But for what purpose? Bah! At any rate, not for the purpose of destroying us. It could have annihilated us much more easily. As far as one can tell, given its technological resources, it could have done anything it wished – confronted me with your double, and you with mine, for example.'

'So that's why you were so alarmed when I arrived, the first evening!'

'Yes. In fact, how do you know it hasn't done so? How do you know I'm really the same old Ratface who landed here two years ago?'

He went on laughing silently, enjoying my discomfiture, then he growled:

'No, no, that's enough of that! We're two happy mortals; I could kill you, you could kill me.'

'And the others, can't they be killed?'

'I don't advise you to try – a horrible sight!'

'Is there no means of killing them?'

'I don't know. Certainly not with poison, or a weapon, or by injection . . .'

'What about a gamma pistol?'

'Would you risk it?'

'Since we know they're not human . . .'

'In a certain subjective sense, they *are* human. They know nothing whatsoever about their origins. You must have noticed that?'

'Yes. But then, how do you explain . . .?'

'They . . . the whole thing is regenerated with extra-ordinary rapidity, at an incredible speed – in the twinkling of an eye. Then they start behaving again as . . .'

'As?'

'As we remember them, as they are engraved on our memories, following which . . .'

'Did Gibarian know?' I interrupted.

'As much as we do, you mean?'

'Yes.'

'Very probably.'

'Did he say anything to you?'

'No. I found a book in his room . . .'

I leapt to my feet.

'*The Little Apocrypha*!'

'Yes.' He looked at me suspiciously. 'Who could have told you about that?'

I shook my head.

'Don't worry, you can see that I've burnt my skin and that it's not exactly renewing itself. No, Gibarian left a letter addressed to me in his cabin.'

'A letter? What did it say?'

'Nothing much. It was more of a note than a letter, with bibliographic references – allusions to the supplement to the *Annual* and to the *Apocrypha*. What is this *Apocrypha*?'

'An antique which seems to have some relevance to our situation. Here!' He drew from his pocket a small, leather-bound volume, scuffed at the edges, and handed it to me.

I grabbed the little book.

'And what about Sartorius?'

'Him! Everyone has his own way of coping. Sartorius is trying to remain normal – that is, to preserve his respectability as an envoy on an official mission.'

'You're joking!'

'No, I'm quite serious. We were together on another occasion. I won't bother you with the details, but there were eight of us and we were down to our last thousand pounds of oxygen. One after another, we gave up our chores, and by the end we all had beards except Sartorius. He was the only one who shaved and polished his shoes. He's like that. Now, of course, he can only pretend, act a part – or else commit a crime.'

'A crime?'

'Perhaps that isn't quite the right word. "Divorce by ejection!" Does that sound better?'

'Very funny!'

'Suggest something else if you don't like it.'

'Oh, leave me alone!'

'No, let's discuss the thing seriously. You know pretty well as much as I do by now. Have you got a plan?'

'No, none. I haven't the least idea what I'll do when . . . when she comes back. She will return, if I've understood you correctly?'

'It's on the cards.'

'How do they get in? The Station is hermetically sealed. Perhaps the layer on the outer hull . . .'

He shook his head.

'The outer hull is in perfect condition. I don't know where they get in. Usually, they're there when you wake up, and you have to sleep eventually!'

'Could you barricade yourself securely inside a cabin?'

'The barricades wouldn't survive for long. There's only one solution, and you can guess what that is . . .'

We both stood up.

'Just a minute, Snow! You're suggesting we liquidate the Station and you expect me to take the initiative and accept the responsibility?'

'It's not as simple as that. Obviously, we could get out, if only as far as the satellite, and send an SOS from there. Of course, we'll be regarded as lunatics; we'll be shut up in a mad-house on Earth – unless we have the sense to retract. A distant planet, isolation, collective derangement – our case won't seem at all out of the ordinary. But at least we'd be better off in a mental home than we are here: a quiet garden, little white cells, nurses, supervised walks . . .'

Hands in his pockets, staring fixedly at a corner of the room, he spoke with the utmost seriousness.

The red sun had disappeared over the horizon and the ocean was a sombre desert, mottled with dying gleams, the last rays lingering among the long tresses of the waves. The sky was ablaze. Purple-edged clouds drifted across this dismal red and black world.

'Well, do you want to get out, yes or no? Or not yet?'

'Always the fighter! If you knew the full implications of what you're asking, you wouldn't be so insistent. It's not a matter of what I want, it's a matter of what's possible.'

'Such as what?'

'That's the point, I don't know.'

'We stay here then? Do you think we'll find some way . . .?'

Thin, sickly looking, his peeling face deeply lined, he turned towards me:

'It might be worth our while to stay. We're unlikely to learn anything about *it*, but about ourselves . . .'

He turned, picked up his papers, and went out. I opened my mouth to detain him, but no sound escaped my lips.

There was nothing I could do now except wait. I went to the window and ran my eyes absently over the dark red glimmer of the shadowed ocean. For a moment, I thought of locking myself inside one of the capsules on the hangar-deck, but it was not an idea worth considering for long: sooner or later, I should have to come out again.

I sat by the window, and began to leaf through the book Snow had given me. The glowing twilight lit up the room and coloured the pages. It was a collection of articles and trea-tises edited by an Otho Ravintzer, Ph.D., and its general level was immediately obvious. Every science engenders some pseudo-science, inspiring eccentrics to explore freakish by-ways; astronomy has its parodists in astrology, chemistry used to have them in alchemy. It was not surprising, there-fore, that Solaristics, in its early days, had set off an explo-sion of marginal cogitations. Ravintzer's book was full of this sort of intellectual speculation, prefaced, it is only fair to add, by an introduction in which the editor dissociated himself from some of the texts reproduced. He considered, with some justice, that such a collection could provide an invalu-able period document as much for the historian as for the psychologist of science.

Berton's report, divided into two parts and complete with a summary of his log, occupied the place of honour in the book.

From 14.00 hours to 16.40 hours, by expedition time, the entries in the log were laconic and negative.

Altitude 3000 – or 3500 – 2500 feet; nothing visible; ocean empty. The same words recurred over and over again.

Then, at 16.40 hours: *A red mist rising. Visibility 700 yards. Ocean empty.*

17.00 hours: fog thickening; visibility 400 yards, with clear patches. Descending to 600 feet.

17.20 hours: in fog. Altitude 600. Visibility 20–40 yards. Climbing to 1200.

17.45: altitude 1500. Pall of fog to horizon. Funnel-shaped open-ings through which I can see ocean surface. Attempting to enter one of these clearings; something is moving.

17.52: have spotted what appears to be a waterspout; it is throwing up a yellow foam. Surrounded by a wall of fog. Altitude 300. Descending to 60 feet.

The extract from Berton's log stopped at this point. There followed his case-history, or, more precisely, the statement dictated by Berton and interrupted at intervals by questions from the members of the Commission of Inquiry.

BERTON: When I reached 100 feet it became very difficult to maintain altitude because of the violent gusts of wind inside the cone. I had to hang on to the controls and for a short period – about ten or fifteen minutes – I did not look outside. I realized too late that a powerful undertow was dragging me back into the fog. It wasn't like an ordinary fog, it was a thick colloidal substance which coated my windows. I had a lot of trouble cleaning them; that fog – or glue rather – was obstinate stuff. Due to this resistance, the speed of my rotor-blades was reduced by 30 per cent and I began losing height. I was afraid of capsizing on the waves; but, even at full power, I could maintain altitude but not increase it. I still had four booster-rockets left but felt the situation was not yet desperate enough to use them. The aircraft was shaken by shuddering vibrations that grew more and more violent. Thinking my rotor-blades must have become coated with the gluey substance, I glanced at the overload indicator, but to my surprise it read zero. Since entering the fog, I had not seen the sun – only a red glow. I continued to fly around in the hope of emerging into one of the funnels, which, after half an hour, was what happened. I found myself in a new 'well', perfectly cylindrical in shape, and several hundred yards in diameter. The walls of the cylinder were formed by an enormous whirlpool of fog, spiralling upwards. I struggled to keep in the middle, where the wind was less violent. It was then that I noticed a change in the ocean's surface. The waves had almost completely disappeared, and the upper layer of the fluid – or whatever the ocean is made of – was becoming transparent, with murky streaks here and there which gradually dissolved until, finally, it was perfectly clear. I could see distinctly to a depth of several yards. I saw a sort of yellow sludge which was sprouting vertical filaments. When these filaments emerged above the surface, they had a glassy sheen. Then they began to exude foam – they frothed – until the foam solidified; it was like a very thick treacle. These glutinous filaments merged and became intertwined; great bubbles swelled up on the surface and slowly began to change shape. Suddenly I realized that my machine was being driven towards the wall of fog. I had to manoeuvre against the wind, and when I was able to look down again, I saw something which looked like a garden. Yes, a garden. Trees, hedges, paths – but it wasn't a real garden; it was all made of the same substance, which had hardened and by now looked like yellow plaster. Beneath this garden, the ocean glittered. I came down as low as I dared in order to take a closer look.

QUESTION: Did the trees and plants you saw have leaves on them?

BERTON: No, the shapes were only approximate, like a model garden. That's exactly what it was like: a model, but lifesize. All of a sudden, it began to crack; it broke up and split into dark crevices; a thick white liquid ran out and collected into pools, or else drained away. The 'earthquake' became more violent, the whole thing boiled over and was buried beneath the foam. At the same time, the walls of the fog began to close in. I gained height rapidly and came clear at 1000 feet.

QUESTION: Are you absolutely sure that what you saw resembled a garden – there was no other possible interpretation?

BERTON: Yes. I noticed several details. For example, I remember seeing a place where there were some boxes in a row. I realized later that they were probably beehives.

QUESTION: You realized later? But not at the time, not at the moment when you actually saw them?

BERTON: No, because everything looked as though it were made of plaster. But I saw something else.

QUESTION: What was that?

BERTON: I saw things which I can't put a name to, because I didn't have time to examine them carefully. Under some bushes I thought I saw tools, long objects with prongs. They might have been plaster models of garden tools. But I'm not absolutely certain. Whereas I'm sure, quite certain, that I recognized an apiary.

QUESTION: It didn't occur to you that it might be a hallucination?

BERTON: No. I thought it was a mirage. It never occurred to me that it was a hallucination because I felt perfectly well, and I had never seen anything like it before. When I reached 1000 feet and took another look at the fog, it was pitted with more irregularly shaped holes, rather like a piece of cheese. Some of these holes were completely hollow, and I could see the ocean waves; others were only shallow saucers in which something was bubbling. I descended another well and saw – the altimeter read 120 feet – I saw a wall lying beneath the ocean surface. It wasn't very deep and I could see it clearly beneath the waves. It seemed to be the wall of a huge building, pierced with rectangular openings, like windows. I even thought I could see something moving behind them, but I couldn't be absolutely certain of that. The wall slowly broke the surface and a mucous bubbling liquid streamed down its sides. Then it suddenly broke in half and disappeared into the depths.

I regained height and continued to fly above the fog, the machine almost touching it, until I discovered another clearing, much larger than the previous one.

While I was still some distance away, I noticed a pale, almost white, object floating on the surface. My first thought was that it was Fechner's flying-suit, especially as it looked vaguely human in form. I brought the aircraft round sharply, afraid of losing my way and being unable to find the same spot again. The shape, the body, was moving; sometimes it seemed to be standing upright in the trough of the waves. I accelerated and went down so low that the machine bounced gently. I must have hit the crest of a huge wave I was over-flying. The body – yes, it was a human body, not an atmosphere suit – the body was moving.

QUESTION: Did you see its face?

BERTON: Yes.

QUESTION: Who was it?

BERTON: A child.

QUESTION: What child? Did you recognize it?

BERTON: No. At any rate, I don't remember having seen it before. Besides, when I got closer – when I was forty yards away, or even sooner – I realized that it was no ordinary child.

QUESTION: What do you mean?

BERTON: I'll explain. At first, I couldn't understand what worried me about it; it was only after a minute or two that I realized: this child was extraordinarily large. Enormous, in fact. Stretched out horizontally, its body rose twelve feet above the surface of the ocean, I swear. I remembered that when I touched the wave, its face was a little higher than mine, even though my cockpit must have been at least ten feet above the ocean.

QUESTION: If it was as big as that, what makes you say it was a child?

BERTON: Because it was a tiny child.

QUESTION: Do you realize, Berton, that your answer doesn't make sense?

BERTON: On the contrary. I could see its face, and it was a very young child. Besides, its proportions corresponded exactly to the proportions of a child's body. It was a . . . babe in arms. No, I exaggerate. It was probably two or three years old. It had black hair and blue eyes – enormous blue eyes! It was naked – completely naked – like a newborn baby. It was wet, or I should say glossy; its skin was shiny. I was shattered. I no longer thought it was a mirage. I could see this child so distinctly. It rose and fell with the waves; but apart from this general motion, it was making other movements, and they were horrible!

QUESTION: Why? What was it doing?

BERTON: It was more like a doll in a museum, only a living doll. It opened and closed its mouth, it made various gestures, horrible gestures.

QUESTION: What do you mean?

BERTON: I was watching it from about twenty yards away – I don't suppose I went any closer. But, as I've already told you, it was enormous. I could see very clearly. Its eyes sparkled and you really would have thought it was a living child, if it hadn't been for the movements, the gestures, as though someone was trying . . . It was as though someone else was responsible for the gestures . . .

QUESTION: Try to be more explicit

BERTON: It's difficult. I'm talking of an impression, more of an intuition. I didn't analyse it, but I knew that those gestures weren't natural.

QUESTION: Do you mean, for example, that the hands didn't move as human hands would move, because the joints were not sufficiently supple?

BERTON: No, not at all. But . . . these movements had no meaning. Each of our movements means something, more or less, serves some purpose . . .

QUESTION: Do you think so? The movements of an infant don't have much meaning!

BERTON: I know. But an infant's movements are confused, random, uncoordinated. The movements I saw were . . . er . . . yes, that's it, they were *methodical* movements. They were performed one after another, like a series of exercises; as though someone had wanted to make a study of what this child was capable of doing with its hands, its torso, its mouth. The face was more horrifying than the rest, because the human face has an expression, and this face ... I don't know how to describe it. It was alive, yes, but it wasn't human. Or rather, the features as a whole, the eyes, the complexion, were, but the expression, the movements of the face, were certainly not.

QUESTION: Were they grimaces? Do you know what happens to a person's face during an epileptic fit?

BERTON: Yes. I've watched an epileptic fit. I know what you mean. No, it was something quite different. Epilepsy provokes spasms, convulsions. The movements I'm talking about were fluid, continuous, graceful ... melodious, if one can say that of a movement. It's the nearest definition I can think of. But this face ... a face can't divide itself into two – one half gay, the other sad, one half scowling and the other amiable, one half frightened and the other triumphant. But that's how it was with this child's face. In addition to that, all these movements and changes of expression succeeded one another with unbelievable rapidity. I stayed down there a very short time, perhaps ten seconds, perhaps less.

QUESTION: And you claim to have seen all that in such a short time? Besides, how do you know how long you were there? Did you check your chronometer?

BERTON: No, but I've been flying for seventeen years and, in my job, one can measure instinctively, to the nearest second, the duration of what would be called an instant of time. It's an acquired faculty, and essential for successful navigation. A pilot isn't worth his salt if he can't tell whether a particular phenomenon lasts five or ten seconds, whatever the circumstances. It's the same with observation. We learn, over the years, to take in everything at a glance.

QUESTION: Is that all you saw?

BERTON: No, but I don't remember the rest so precisely. I suppose I must already have seen more than enough; my attention faltered. The fog began to close in, and I had to climb. I climbed, and for the first time in my life I all but capsized. My hands were shaking so much that I had difficulty in handling the controls. I think I shouted something, called up the base, even though I knew we were not in radio contact.

QUESTION: Did you then try to get back?

BERTON: No. In the end, having gained height, I thought to myself that Fechner was probably in the bottom of one of the wells. I know it sounds crazy, but that's what I thought. I told myself that everything was possible, and that it would also be possible for me to find Fechner. I decided to investigate every clearing I came across along my route. At the third attempt I gave up. When I had regained height, I knew it was useless to persist after what I had just seen on this, the third, occasion. I couldn't go on any longer. I should add, as you already know, that I was suffering from bouts of nausea and that I vomited in the cockpit. I couldn't understand it; I have never been sick in my life.

COMMENT: It was a symptom of poisoning.

BERTON: Perhaps. I don't know. But what I saw on this third occasion I did not imagine. That was not the effect of poisoning.

QUESTION: How can you possibly know?

BERTON: It wasn't a hallucination. A hallucination is created by one's own brain, wouldn't you say?

COMMENT: Yes.

BERTON: Well, my brain couldn't have created what I saw. I'll never believe that. My brain wouldn't have been capable of it.

COMMENT: Get on with describing what it was!

BERTON: Before I do so, I should like to know how the statements I've already made will be interpreted.

QUESTION: What does that matter?

BERTON: For me, it matters very much indeed. I have said that I saw things which I shall never forget. If the Commission recognizes, even with certain reservations, that my testimony is credible, and that a study of the ocean must be

88

undertaken – I mean a study orientated in the light of my statements – then I'll tell everything. But if the Commission considers that it is all delusions, then I refuse to say anything more.

QUESTION: Why?

BERTON: Because the contents of my hallucinations belong to me and I don't have to give an account of them, whereas I am obliged to give an account of what I saw on Solaris.

QUESTION: Does that mean that you refuse to answer any more questions until the expedition authorities have announced their findings? You realize, of course, that the Commission isn't empowered to take an immediate decision?

BERTON: Yes.

The first minute ended here. There followed a fragment of the second minute drawn up eleven days later.

PRESIDENT: ... after due consideration, the Commission, composed of three doctors, three biologists, a physicist, a mechanical engineer and the deputy head of the expedition, has reached the conclusion that Berton's report is symptomatic of hallucinations caused by atmospheric poisoning, consequent upon inflammation of the associative zone of the cerebral cortex, and that Berton's account bears no, or at any rate no appreciable, relation to reality.

BERTON: Excuse me, what does 'no appreciable relation' mean? In what proportion is reality appreciable or not?

PRESIDENT: I haven't finished. Independently of these conclusions, the Commission has duly registered a dissenting vote from Dr Archibald Messenger, who considers the phenomena described by Berton to be objectively possible and declares himself in favour of a scrupulous investigation.

BERTON: I repeat my question.

PRESIDENT: The answer is simple. 'No appreciable relation to reality' means that phenomena actually observed may have formed the basis of your hallucinations. In the course of a nocturnal stroll, a perfectly sane man can imagine he sees a living creature in a bush stirred by the wind. Such illusions are all the more likely to affect an explorer lost on a strange planet and breathing a poisonous atmosphere. This verdict is in no way prejudicial to you, Berton. Will you now be good enough to let us know your decision?

BERTON: First of all, I should like to know the possible consequences of this dissenting vote of Dr Messenger's.

PRESIDENT: Virtually none. We shall carry on our work along the lines originally laid down.

BERTON: Is our interview on record?

PRESIDENT: Yes.

BERTON: In that case, I should like to say that although the Commission's decision may not be prejudicial to me personally, it is prejudicial to the spirit of the expedition itself. Consequently, as I have already stated, I refuse to answer any further questions.

PRESIDENT: Is that all?

BERTON: Yes. Except that I should like to meet Dr Messenger. Is that possible?

PRESIDENT: Of course.

That was the end of the second minute. At the bottom of the page there was a note in minuscule handwriting to the effect that, the following day, Dr Messenger had talked to Berton for nearly three hours. As a result of this conversation, Messenger had once more begged the expedition Council to undertake further investigations in order to check the pilot's statements. Berton had produced some new and extremely convincing revelations, which Messenger could not divulge unless the Council reversed its negative decision. The Council – Shannahan, Timolis and Trahier – rejected the motion and the affair was closed.

The book also reproduced a photocopy of the last page of a letter, or rather, the draft of a letter, found by Messenger's executors after his death. Ravintzer, in spite of his researches, had been unable to discover if this letter had ever been sent.

'. . . obtuse minds, a pyramid of stupidity' – the text began. 'Anxious to preserve its authority, the Council – more precisely Shannahan and Timolis (Trahier's vote doesn't count) – has rejected my recommendations. Now I am taking the matter up directly with the Institute; but, as you can well imagine, my protestations won't convince anybody. Bound as I am by oath, I can't, alas, reveal to you what Berton told me. If the Council disregarded Berton's testimony, it was basically because Berton has no scientific training, although any scientist would envy the presence of mind and the gift of observation shown by this pilot. I should be grateful if you could send me the following information by return post:

i) Fechner's biography, in particular details about his childhood.

ii) Everything you know about his family, facts and dates – he probably lost his parents while still a child.

iii) The topography of the place where he was brought up.

'I should like once more to tell you what I think about all this. As you know, some time after the departure of Fechner and Carucci, a spot appeared in the centre of the red sun. This chromospheric eruption caused a magnetic storm chiefly over the southern hemisphere, where our base was situated, according to the information provided by the satellite, and the radio links were cut. The other parties were scouring the planet's surface over a relatively restricted area, whereas Fechner and Carucci had travelled a considerable distance from the base.

'Never, since our arrival on the planet, had we observed such a persistent fog or such an unremitting silence.

'I imagine that what Berton saw was one of the phases of a kind of "Operation Man" which this viscous monster was engaged in. The source of all the various forms observed by Berton is Fechner – or rather, Fechner's brain, subjected to an unimaginable "psychic dissection" for the purposes of a sort of re-creation, an experimental reconstruction, based on impressions (undoubtedly the most durable ones) engraved on his memory.

'I know this sounds fantastic; I know that I may be mistaken. But do please help me. At the moment, I am on the *Alaric*, where I look forward to receiving your reply.

Yours,

A.'

It was a growing dark, and I could scarcely make out the blurred print at the top of the grey page – the last page describing Berton's adventure. For my part, my own experience led me to regard Berton as a trustworthy witness.

I turned towards the window. A few clouds still glowed like dying embers above the horizon. The ocean was invisible, blanketed by the purple darkness.

The strips of paper fluttered idly beneath the air-vents. There was a whiff of ozone in the still, warm air.

There was nothing heroic in our decision to remain on the Station. The time for heroism was over, vanished with the era of the great interplanetary triumphs, of daring expeditions and sacrifices. Fechner, the ocean's first victim, belonged to a distant past. I had almost stopped caring about the identity of Snow's and Sartorius's visitors. Soon, I told myself, we would cease to be ashamed, to keep ourselves apart. If we could not get rid of our visitors, we would accustom ourselves to their presence, learn to live with them. If their Creator altered the rules of the game, we would adapt ourselves to the new rules, even if at first we jibbed or rebelled, even if one of us despaired and killed himself. Eventually, a certain equilibrium would be re-established.

Night had come; no different from many nights on Earth. Now I could make out only the white contours of the basin and the smooth surface of the mirror.

I stood up. Groping my way to the basin, I fumbled among the objects which cluttered up the shelf, and found the packet of cotton-wool. I washed my face with a damp wad and stretched out on the bed.

A moth fluttered its wings ... no, it was the ventilator-strip. The whirring stopped, then started up again. I could no longer see the window; everything had merged into darkness. A mysterious ray of light pierced the blackness and lingered in front of me – against the wall, or the black sky? I remembered how the blank stare of the night had frightened me the day before, and I smiled at the thought. I was no longer afraid of the night; I was not afraid of anything. I raised my wrist and looked at the ring of phosphorescent figures; another hour, and the blue day would dawn.

I breathed deeply, savouring the darkness, my mind empty and at rest.

Shifting my position, I felt the flat shape of the tape-recorder against my hip: Gibarian, his voice immortalized on the spools of tape. I had forgotten to resurrect him, to listen to him – the only thing I could do for him any more. I took the tape-recorder out of my pocket in order to hide it under the bed.

I heard a rustling sound; the door opened.

'Kris?' An anxious voice whispered my name. 'Kris, are you there? It's so dark . . .'

I answered:

'Yes, I'm here. Don't be frightened, come!'

The Conference

I was lying on my back, with Rheya's head resting on my shoulder.

The darkness was peopled now. I could hear footsteps. Something was piling up above me, higher and higher, infinitely high. The night transfixed me; the night took possession of me, enveloped and penetrated me, impalpable, insubstantial. Turned to stone, I had ceased breathing, there was no air to breathe. As though from a distance, I heard the beating of my heart. I summoned up all my remaining strength, straining every nerve, and waited for death. I went on waiting . . . I seemed to be growing smaller, and the invisible sky, horizonless, the formless immensity of space, without clouds, without stars, receded, extended and grew bigger all round me. I tried to crawl out of bed, but there was no bed; beneath the cover of darkness there was a void. I pressed my hands to my face. I no longer had any fingers or any hands. I wanted to scream . . .

The room floated in a blue penumbra, which outlined the furniture and the laden bookshelves, and drained everything of colour. A pearly whiteness flooded the window.

I was drenched with sweat. I glanced to one side. Rheya was gazing at me.

She raised her head.

'Has your arm gone to sleep?'

Her eyes too had been drained of colour; they were grey, but luminous, beneath the black lashes.

'What?' Her murmured words had seemed like a caress even before I understood their meaning. 'No. Ah, yes!' I said, at last.

I put my hand on her shoulder; I had pins and needles in my fingers.

'Did you have a bad dream?' she asked.

I drew her to me with my other hand.

'A dream? Yes, I was dreaming. And you, didn't you sleep?'

'I don't know. I don't think so. I'm sleepy. But that mustn't stop you from sleeping ... Why are you looking at me like that?'

I closed my eyes. Her heart was beating against mine. Her heart? A mere appendage, I told myself. But nothing surprised me any longer, not even my own indifference. I had crossed the frontiers of fear and despair. I had come a long way – further than anyone had ever come before.

I raised myself on my elbow. Daybreak ... and the peace that comes with dawn? A silent storm had set the cloudless horizon ablaze. A streak of light, the first ray of the blue sun, penetrated the room and broke up into sharp-edged reflections; there was a crossfire of sparks, which coruscated off the mirror, the door-handles, the nickel pipes. The light scattered, falling on to every smooth surface as though it wanted to conquer ever more space, to set the room alight. I looked at Rheya; the pupils of her grey eyes had contracted.

She asked in an expressionless voice, 'Is the night over already?'

'Night never lasts long here.'

'And us?'

'What about us?'

'Are we going to stay here long?'

Coming from her, the question had its comic side; but when I spoke, my voice held no trace of gaiety.

'Quite a long time, probably. Why, don't you want to stay here?'

Her eyes did not blink. She was looking at me enquiringly. Did I see her blink? I was not sure. She drew back the blanket and I saw the little pink scar on her arm.

'Why are you looking at me like that?'

'Because you're very beautiful.'

She smiled, without a trace of mischief, modestly acknowledging my compliment.

'Really? It's as though . . . as though . . .'

'What?'

'As though you were doubtful of something.'

'What nonsense!'

'As though you didn't trust me and I were hiding something from you . . .'

'Rubbish!'

'By the way you're denying it, I can tell I'm right.'

The light became blinding. Shading my eyes with my hand, I looked for my dark glasses. They were on the table. When I was back by her side, Rheya smiled.

'What about me?'

It took me a minute to understand what she meant.

'Dark glasses?'

I got up and began to hunt through drawers and shelves, pushing aside books and instruments. I found two pairs of glasses, which I gave to Rheya. They were too big; they fell halfway down her nose.

The shutters slid over the window; it was dark once more. Groping, I helped Rheya remove her glasses and put both pairs down under the bed.

'What shall we do now?' she asked.

'At night-time, one sleeps!'

'Kris . . .'

'Yes?'

'Do you want a compress for your forehead?'

'No, thanks. Thank you . . . my darling.'

I don't know why I had added those two words. In the darkness, I took her by her graceful shoulders. I felt them tremble, and I knew, without the least shadow of doubt, that I held Rheya in my arms. Or rather, I understood in that moment that she was not trying to deceive me; it was I who was deceiving her, since she sincerely believed herself to be Rheya.

I dropped off several times after that, and each time an anguished start jolted me awake. Panting, exhausted, I pressed myself closer to her; my heart gradually growing calmer. She touched me cautiously on the cheeks and forehead with the tips of her fingers, to see whether or not I was feverish. It was Rheya, the real Rheya, the one and only Rheya.

A change came over me; I ceased to struggle and almost at once I fell asleep.

I was awakened by an agreeable sensation of coolness. My face was covered by a damp cloth. I pulled it off and found Rheya leaning over me. She was smiling and squeezing out a second cloth over a bowl.

'What a sleep!' she said, laying another compress on my forehead. 'Are you ill?'

'No.'

I wrinkled my forehead; the skin was supple once again. Rheya sat on the edge of my bed, her black hair brushed back over the collar of a bathrobe – a man's bathrobe, with orange and black stripes, the sleeves turned back to the elbow.

I was terribly hungry; it was at least twenty hours since my last meal. When Rheya had finished her ministrations I got up. Two dresses, draped over the back of a chair, caught my eye – two absolutely identical white dresses, each decorated with a row of red buttons. I myself had helped Rheya out of one of them, and she had reappeared, yesterday evening, dressed in the second.

She followed my glance.

'I had to cut the seam open with scissors,' she said. 'I think the zip-fastener must have got stuck.'

The sight of the two identical dresses filled me with a horror which exceeded anything I had felt hitherto. Rheya was busy tidying up the medicine chest. I turned my back and bit my knuckles. Unable to take my eyes off the two dresses – or rather the original dress and its double – I backed towards the door. The basin tap was running noisily. I opened the door and, slipping out of the room, cautiously closed it behind me. I heard the sound of running water, the clinking of bottles; then, suddenly, all sound ceased. I waited, my jaw clenched, my hands gripping the door handle, but with little hope of holding it shut. It was nearly torn from my grasp by a savage jerk. But the door did not open; it shook and vibrated from top to bottom. Dazed, I let go of the handle and stepped back. The panel, made of some plastic material, caved in as though an invisible person at my side had tried to break into the room. The steel frame bent further and further inwards and the paint was cracking. Suddenly I understood: instead of pushing the door, which opened outwards, Rheya was trying to open it by pulling it towards her. The reflection of the lighting strip in the ceiling was distorted in the white-painted door-panel; there was a resounding crack and the panel, forced beyond its limits, gave way. Simultaneously the handle vanished, torn from its mounting. Two bloodstained hands appeared, thrusting through the opening and smearing the white paint with blood. The door split in two, the broken halves hanging askew on their hinges. First a face appeared, deathly pale, then a wild-looking apparition, dressed in an orange and black bathrobe, flung itself sobbing upon my chest.

I wanted to escape, but it was too late, and I was rooted to the spot. Rheya was breathing convulsively, her dishevelled head drumming against my chest. Before I could put my arms round her to hold her up, Rheya collapsed.

Avoiding the ragged edges of the broken panel, I carried her into the room and laid her on the bed. Her fingertips were grazed and the nails torn. When her hands turned upwards, I saw that the palms were cut to the bone. I examined her face; her glazed eyes showed no sign of recognition.

'Rheya.'

The only answer was an inarticulate groan.

I went over to the medicine chest. The bed creaked; I turned round; Rheya was sitting up, looking at her bleeding hands with astonishment.

'Kris,' she sobbed, 'I . . . I . . . what happened to me?'

'You hurt yourself trying to break down the door,' I answered curtly.

My lips were twitching convulsively, and I had to bite the lower one to keep it under control.

Rheya's glance took in the pieces of door-panel hanging from the steel frame, then she turned her eyes back towards me. She was doing her best to hide her terror, but I could see her chin trembling.

I cut off some squares of gauze, picked up a pot of antiseptic powder and returned to the bedside. The glass jar slipped through my hands and shattered – but I no longer needed it.

I lifted one of Rheya's hands. The nails, still surrounded by traces of clotted blood, had regrown. There was a pink scar in the hollow of her palm, but even this scar was healing, disappearing in front of my eyes.

I sat beside her and stroked her face, trying to smile without much success.

'What did you do that for, Rheya?'

'I did . . . that?'

With her eyes, she indicated the door.

'Yes . . . Don't you remember?'

'No . . . that is, I saw you weren't there, I was very frightened, and . . .'

'And what?'

'I looked for you. I thought that perhaps you were in the bathroom . . .'

Only then did I notice that the sliding door covering the entrance to the bathroom had been pushed back.

'And then?'

'I ran to the door.'

'And after that?'

99

'I can't remember . . . Something must have happened . . .'

'What?'

'I don't know.'

'What do you remember?'

'I was sitting here, on the bed.'

She swung her legs over the edge of the bed, got up and went over to the shattered door.

'Kris!'

Walking up behind her, I took her by the shoulders; she was shaking. She suddenly turned and whispered:

'Kris, Kris . . .'

'Calm yourself!'

'Kris, if it's me . . . Kris, am I an epileptic?'

'What an extraordinary idea, my sweet. The doors in this place are rather special . . .'

We left the room as the shutter was grinding its way up the window; the blue sun was sinking into the ocean.

I guided Rheya to the small kitchen on the other side of the dome. Together we raided the cupboards and the refrigerators. I soon noticed that Rheya was scarcely better than I was at cooking or even at opening tins. I devoured the contents of two tins and drank innumerable cups of coffee. Rheya also ate, but as children eat when they are not hungry and do not want to displease their parents; on the other hand, she was not forcing herself, simply taking in nourishment automatically, indifferently.

After our meal, we went into the sick bay, next to the radio-cabin. I had had an idea. I told Rheya that I wanted to give her a medical examination – a straightforward checkup – sat her in a mechanical chair, and took a syringe and some needles out of the sterilizer. I knew exactly where each object was to be found; as far as the model of the Station's interior was concerned, the instructors had not overlooked a single detail during my training course. Rheya held out her fingers; I took a sample of blood. I smeared the blood on to a slide which I laid in the suction pipe, introduced it into the vacuum tank and bombarded it with silver ions.

Performing a familiar task had a soothing effect, and I felt better. Rheya, leaning back on the cushions in the mechanical chair, gazed around at the instruments in the sick bay.

The buzzing of the videophone broke the silence; I lifted the receiver:

'Kelvin.'

I looked at Rheya; she was still quiet, apparently exhausted by her recent efforts.

I heard a sigh of relief.

'At last.'

It was Snow. I waited, the receiver pressed close to my ear.

'You've had a visit, haven't you?'

'Yes.'

'Are you busy?'

'Yes.'

'A little auscultation, eh?'

"I suppose you've got a better suggestion – a game of chess maybe?'

'Don't be so touchy, Kelvin! Sartorius wants to meet you, he wants all three of us to meet.'

'Very kind of him!' I answered, taken aback. 'But . . .' I stopped, then went on: 'Is he alone?'

'No. I haven't explained properly. He wants to have a talk with us. We'll set up a three-way videophone link, but with the telescreen lenses covered.'

'I see. Why didn't he contact me himself? Is he frightened of me?'

'Quite possibly,' grunted Snow. 'What do you say?'

'A conference. In an hour's time. Will that suit you?'

'That's fine.'

I could see him on the screen – just his face, about the size of a fist. For a moment, he looked at me attentively; I could hear the crackling of the electric current. Then he said, hesitantly:

'Are you getting on all right?'

'Not too bad. How about you?'

'Not so well as you, I dare say. May I . . .?'

'Do you want to come over here?'

I glanced at Rheya over my shoulder. She was leaning back, legs crossed, her head bent. With a morose air, she was fiddling mechanically with the little chrome ball on the end of a chain fixed to the arm-rest.

Snow's voice erupted:

'Stop that, do you hear? I told you to stop it!'

I could see his profile on the screen, but I could no longer hear him although his lips were moving – he had put his hand over the microphone.

'No, I can't come,' he said quickly. 'Later perhaps, in any case, I'll contact you in an hour.'

The screen went blank; I replaced the receiver.

'Who was it?' asked Rheya indifferently.

'Snow, a cybernetician. You don't know him.'

'Is this going on much longer?'

'Are you bored?'

I put the first of the series of slides into the neutron microscope, and, one after another, I pressed the different-coloured switches; the magnetic fields rumbled hollowly.

'There's not much to do in here, and if my humble company isn't enough for you . . .'

I was talking distractedly, with long gaps between my words.

I pulled the big black hood round the eye-piece of the microscope towards me, and leant my forehead against the resilient foam-rubber viewer. I could hear Rheya's voice, but without taking in what she was saying. Beneath my gaze, sharply foreshortened, was a vast desert flooded with silvery light, and strewn with rounded boulders – red corpuscles – which trembled and wriggled behind a veil of mist. I focused the eye-piece and penetrated further into the depths of the silvery landscape. Without taking my eyes away from the viewer, I turned the view-finder; when a boulder, a single corpuscle, detached itself and appeared at the junction of the cross-hairs, I enlarged the image. The lens had apparently picked up a deformed erythrocyte, sunken in the centre, whose uneven edges projected sharp shadows over the depths of a circular crater. The crater, bristling with silver ion deposits, extended beyond the microscope's field of vision. The nebulous outlines of threads of albumen, distorted and atrophied, appeared in the midst of an opalescent liquid. A worm of albumen twisted and turned beneath the cross-hairs of the lens. Gradually I increased the enlargement. At any moment, I should reach the limit of this exploration of the depths; the shadow of a molecule occupied the whole of the space; then the image became fuzzy.

There was nothing to be seen. There should have been the ferment of a quivering cloud of atoms, but I saw nothing. A dazzling light filled the screen, which was flawlessly clear. I pushed the lever to its utmost. The angry, whirring noise grew louder, but the screen remained a blank. An alarm signal sounded once, then was repeated; the circuit was overloaded. I took a final look at the silvery desert, then I cut the current.

I looked at Rheya. She was in the middle of a yawn which she changed adroitly into a smile.

'Am I in good health?' she asked.

'Excellent. Couldn't be better.'

I continued to look at her and once more I felt as though something was crawling along my lower lip. What had happened exactly? What was the meaning of it? Was this body, frail and weak in appearance but indestructible in reality, actually made of nothing? I gave the microscope cylinder a blow with my fist. Was the instrument out of order? No, I knew that it was working perfectly. I had followed the procedure faithfully: first the cells, then the albumen, then the molecules; and everything was just as I was accustomed to seeing it in the course of examining thousands of slides. But the final step, into the heart of the matter, had taken me nowhere.

I put a ligature on Rheya, took some blood from a median vein and transferred it to a graduated glass, then divided it between several test-tubes and began the analyses. These took longer than usual; I was rather out of practice. The reactions were normal, every one of them.

I dropped some congealed acid on to a coral-tinted pearl. Smoke. The blood turned grey and a dirty foam rose to the surface. Disintegration, decomposition, faster and faster! I turned my back to get another test-tube; when I looked again at the experiment, I nearly dropped the slim glass phial.

Beneath the skin of dirty foam, a dark coral was rising. The blood, destroyed by the acid, was re-creating itself. It was crazy, impossible!

'Kris.' I heard my name called, as though from a great distance. 'Kris, the videophone!'

'What? Oh, thanks.'

The instrument had been buzzing for some time, but I had only just noticed it.

I picked up the receiver:

'Kelvin.'

'Snow. We are now all three plugged into the same circuit.'

The high-pitched voice of Sartorius came over the receiver:

'Greetings, Dr Kelvin!' It was the wary tone of voice, full of false assurance, of the lecturer who knows he is on tenuous ground.

'Good-day to you, Dr Sartorius!'

I wanted to laugh; but in the circumstances I hardly felt I could yield to a mood of hilarity. After all, which of us was the laughing stock? In my hand I held a test-tube containing some blood. I shook it. The blood coagulated. Had I been the victim of an illusion a moment ago? Had I, perhaps, been mistaken?

'I should like to set forth, gentlemen, certain questions concerning the . . . the phantoms.'

I listened to Sartorius, but my mind refused to take in his words. I was pondering the coagulated blood and shutting out this distracting voice.

'Let's call them Phi-creatures,' Snow interjected.

'Very well, agreed.'

A vertical line, bisecting the screen and barely perceptible, showed that I was linked to two channels: on either side of this line, I should have seen two images – Snow and Sartorius. But the light-rimmed screen remained dark. Both my interlocutors had covered the lenses of their sets.

'Each of us has made various experiments.' The nasal voice still held the same wariness. There was a pause.

'I suggest first of all that we pool such knowledge as we have acquired so far,' Sartorius went on. 'Afterwards, I shall venture to communicate to you the conclusions that I, personally, have reached. If you would be so good as to begin, Dr Kelvin . . .'

'Me?'

All of a sudden, I sensed Rheya watching me. I put my hand on the table and rolled the test-tube under the instrument racks. Then I perched myself on a stool which I dragged up with my foot. I was about to decline to give an opinion when, to my surprise, I heard myself answer:

'Right. A little talk? I haven't done much, but I can tell you about it. A histological sample . . . certain reactions. Microreactions. I have the impression that . . .' I did not know how to go on. Suddenly I found my tongue and continued: 'Everything looks normal, but it's a camouflage. A cover. In a way, it's a super-copy, a reproduction which is superior to the original. I'll explain what I mean: there exists, in man, an absolute limit – a term to structural divisibility – whereas here, the frontiers have been pushed back. We are dealing with a sub-atomic structure.'

'Just a minute, just a minute! Kindly be more precise!' Sartorius interrupted.

Snow said nothing. Did I catch an echo of his rapid breathing? Rheya was looking at me again. I realized that, in my excitement, I had almost shouted the last words. Calmer, I settled myself on my uncomfortable perch and closed my eyes. How could I be more precise?

'The atom is the ultimate constituent element of our bodies. My guess is that the Phi-beings are constituted of units smaller than ordinary atoms, much smaller.'

'Mesons,' put in Sartorius. He did not sound in the least surprised.

'No, not mesons . . . I would have seen them. The power of this instrument here is between a tenth and a twentieth of an angstrom, isn't it? But nothing is visible, nothing whatsoever. So it can't be mesons. More likely neutrinos.'

'How do you account for that theory? Conglomerations of neutrinos are unstable . . .'

'I don't know. I'm not a physicist. Perhaps a magnetic field could stabilize them. It's not my province. In any event, if my observations are correct, the structure is made up of particles at least ten thousand times smaller than atoms. Wait a minute, I haven't finished! If the albuminous molecules and the cells were directly constructed from micro-atoms, they must be proportionally even smaller. This applies to the corpuscles, the micro-organisms, everything. Now, the dimensions are those of atomic structures. Consequently, the albumen, the cell and the nucleus of the cell are nothing but camouflage. The real structure, which determines the functions of the visitor, remains concealed.'

'Kelvin!'

Snow had uttered a stifled cry. I stopped, horrified. I had said 'visitor'.

Rheya had not overheard. At any rate, she had not understood. Her head in her hand, she was staring out of the window, her delicate profile etched against the purple dawn.

My distant interlocutors were silent; I could hear their breathing.

'There's something in what he says,' Snow muttered.

'Yes,' remarked Sartorius, 'but for one fact: Kelvin's hypothetical particles have nothing to do with the structure of the ocean. The ocean is composed of atoms.'

'Perhaps it's capable of producing neutrinos,' I replied.

Suddenly I was bored with all their talk. The conversation was pointless, and not even amusing.

'Kelvin's hypothesis explains this extraordinary resistance and the speed of regeneration,' Snow growled. 'They probably carry their own energy source as well; they don't need food . . .'

'I believe I have the chair,' Sartorius interrupted. The self-designated chairman of the debate was clinging exasperatingly to his role. 'I should like to raise the question of the motivation behind the appearance of the Phi-creatures. I put it to you as follows: what are the Phi-creatures? They are not autonomous individuals, nor copies of actual persons. They are merely projections materializing from our brains, based on a given individual.'

I was struck by the soundness of this description; Sartorius might not be very sympathetic, but he was certainly no fool.

I rejoined the conversation:

'I think you're right. Your definition explains why a particular per . . . creation appears rather than another. The origin of the materialization lies in the most durable imprints of memory, those which are especially well defined, but no single imprint can be completely isolated, and in the course of the reproduction, fragments of related imprints are absorbed. Thus the new arrival sometimes reveals a more extensive knowledge than that of the individual of whom it is a copy . . .'

'Kelvin!' shouted Snow once more.

It was only Snow who reacted to my lapses; Sartorius did not seem to be affected by them. Did this mean that Sartorius's visitor was less perspicacious than Snow's? For a moment, I imagined the scholarly Sartorius cohabiting with a cretinous dwarf.

'Indeed, that corresponds with our observations,' Sartorius said. 'Now, let us consider the motivation behind the apparition! It is natural enough to assume, in the first instance, that we are the object of an experiment. When I examine this proposition, the experiment seems to me badly designed. When we carry out an experiment, we profit by the results and, above all, we carefully note the defects of our methods. As a result, we introduce modifications in our future procedure. But, in the case with which we are concerned, not a single modification has occurred. The Phi-creatures reappear exactly as they were, down to the last detail . . . as vulnerable as before, each time we attempt to . . . to rid ourselves of them.'

'Exactly,' I broke in, 'a recoil, with no compensating mechanism, as Dr Snow would say. Conclusions?'

'Simply that the thesis of experimentation is inconsistent with this . . . this unbelievable bungling. The ocean is . . . precise. The dual-level structure of the Phi-creatures testifies to this precision. Within the prescribed limits, the Phi-creatures behave in the same way as the real . . . the . . . er . . .'

He could not disentangle himself.

'The originals,' said Snow, in a loud whisper.

'Yes, the originals. But when the situation no longer corresponds to the normal faculties of . . . er . . . the original, the Phi-creature suffers a sort of "disconnection of consciousness", followed immediately by unusual, non-human manifestations . . .'

'It's true,' I said, 'and we can amuse ourselves drawing up a catalogue of the behaviour of . . . of these creatures – a totally frivolous occupation!'

'I'm not so sure of that,' protested Sartorius. I suddenly realized why he irritated me so much: he didn't talk, he lectured, as though he were in the chair at the Institute. He seemed to be incapable of expressing himself in any other way. 'Here we come to the question of individuality,' he went on, 'of which, I am quite sure, the ocean has not the smallest inkling. I think that the ... er ... delicate or shocking aspect of our present situation is completely beyond its comprehension.'

'You think its activities are unpremeditated?'

I was somewhat bewildered by Sartorius's point of view, but on second thought, I realized that it could not be dismissed.

'No, unlike our colleague Snow, I don't believe there is malice, or deliberate cruelty ...'

Snow broke in:

'I'm not suggesting it has human feelings, I'm merely trying to find an explanation for these continual reappearances.'

With a secret desire to nag poor Sartorius, I said:

'Perhaps they are plugged into a contrivance which goes round and round, endlessly repeating itself, like a gramophone record ...'

'Gentlemen, I beg you, let us not waste time! I haven't yet finished. In normal circumstances, I would have felt it premature to present a report, even a provisional one, on the progress of my research; in view of the prevailing situation, however, I think I may allow myself to speak out. I have the impression – only an impression, mark you – that Dr Kelvin's hypothesis is not without validity. I am alluding to the hypothesis of a neutrino structure ... Our knowledge in this field is purely theoretical. We did not know if there was any possibility of stabilizing such structures. Now a clearly defined solution offers itself to us. A means of neutralizing the magnetic field that maintains the stability of the structure ...'

A few moments previously, I had noticed that the screen was flickering with light. Now a split appeared from top to bottom of the left-hand side. I saw something pink move slowly out of view. Then the lens-cover slipped again, disclosing the screen.

Sartorius gave an anguished cry:

'Go away! Go away!'

I saw his hands flapping and struggling, then his fore-arms, covered by the wide sleeves of the laboratory gown. A bright golden disc shone out for an instant, then everything went dark. Only then did I realize that this golden disc was a straw hat . . .

I took a deep breath.

'Snow?'

An exhausted voice replied:

'Yes, Kelvin . . .' Hearing his voice, I realized that I had become quite fond of him, and that I preferred not to know who or what his companion was. 'That's enough for now, don't you think?' he said.

'I agree.' Before he could cut off, I added quickly: 'Listen, if you can, come and see me, either in the operating room or in my cabin.'

'OK, but I don't know when.'

The conference was over.

The Monsters

I woke up in the middle of the night to find the light on and Rheya crouched at the end of the bed, wrapped in a sheet, her shoulders shaking with silent tears. I called her name and asked her what was wrong, but she only curled up tighter.

Still half asleep, and barely emerged from the nightmare which had been tormenting me only a moment before, I pulled myself up to a sitting position and shielded my eyes against the glare to look at her. The trembling continued, and I stretched out my arms, but Rheya pushed me away and hid her face.

'Rheya . . .'

'Don't talk to me!'

'Rheya, what's the matter?'

I caught a glimpse of her tear-stained face, contorted with emotion. The big childish tears streamed down her face, glistened in the dimple above her chin and fell on to the sheet.

'You don't want me.'

'What are you talking about?'

'I heard . . .'

My jaw tightened:

'Heard what? You don't understand . . .'

'Yes I do. You said I wasn't Rheya. You wanted me to go, and I would, I really would . . . but I can't. I don't know why. I've tried to go, but I couldn't do it. I'm such a coward.'

'Come on now . . .' I put my arms round her and held her with all my strength. Nothing mattered to me except her: everything else was meaningless. I kissed her hands, talked, begged, excused myself and made promise after promise, saying that she had been having some silly, terrible dream.

111

Gradually she grew calmer, and at last she stopped crying and her eyes glazed, like a woman walking in her sleep. She turned her face away from me.

'No,' she said at last, 'be quiet, don't talk like that. It's no good, you're not the same person any more.' I started to protest, but she went on: 'No, you don't want me. I knew it before, but I pretended not to notice. I thought perhaps I was imagining everything, but it was true . . . you've changed. You're not being honest with me. You talk about dreams, but it was you who were dreaming, and it was to do with me. You spoke my name as if it repelled you. Why? Just tell me why.'

'Rheya, my little . . .'

'I won't have you talking to me like that, do you hear? I won't let you. I'm not your little anything, I'm not a child. I'm . . .'

She burst into tears and buried her face in the pillow. I got up. The ventilation hummed quietly. It was cold, and I pulled a dressing-gown over my shoulders before sitting next to her and taking her arm: 'Listen to me, I'm going to tell you something. I'm going to tell you the truth.'

She pushed herself upright again. I could see the veins throbbing beneath the delicate skin of her neck. My jaw tightened once more. The air seemed to be colder still, and my head was completely empty.

'The truth?' she said. 'Word of honour?'

I opened my mouth to speak, but no sound came. 'Word of honour' . . . it was our special catch-phrase, our old way of making an unconditional promise. Once these words had been spoken, neither of us was permitted to lie, or even to take refuge behind a half-truth. I remembered the period when we used to torture each other in an exaggerated striving for sincerity, convinced that this ingenuous honesty was the precondition of our relationship.

'Word of honour, Rheya,' I answered gravely, and she waited for me to continue. 'You have changed too – we all change. But that is not what I wanted to say. For some reason that neither of us understands, it seems that ... you are forced to stay near me. And that's fine with me, because I can't leave you either ...'

'No, Kris. The change is not in you,' Rheya whispered. 'It's me. Something is wrong. Perhaps it has to do with the accident?'

She looked at the dark, empty rectangle of the door. The previous evening, I had removed the shattered remains – a new one would have to be fitted. Another thought struck me:

'Have you been managing to sleep?'

'I don't know.'

'What do you mean?'

'I have dreams ... I don't know whether they really are dreams. Perhaps I'm ill. I lie there and think, and ...'

'What?'

'I have strange thoughts. I don't know where they come from.'

It took all my self-control to steady my voice and tell her to go on, and I found myself tensing for her answer as if for a blow in the face.

'They are thoughts ...' She shook her head helplessly. '... all around me.'

'I don't understand.'

'I get a feeling as if they were not from inside myself, but somewhere further away. I can't explain it, can't put words to it ...'

I broke in almost involuntarily:

'It must be some kind of dream.' Then, back in control again: 'And now, we put the light out and we forget our problems until morning. Tomorrow we can invent some new ones if you like. OK?'

She pressed the switch, and darkness fell between us. Stretched out on the bed, I felt her warm breathing beside me, and put my arms round her.

'Harder!' she whispered, and then, after a long pause:

'Kris!'

'What?'

'I love you.'

I almost screamed.

In the red morning, the sun's swollen disc was rising over the horizon.

An envelope lay in the doorway, and I tore it open. I could hear Rheya humming to herself in the bath, and from time to time she looked into the room and I would see her face, half hidden by her wet hair.

I went to the window, and read:

Kelvin, things are looking up. Sartorius has decided that it may be possible to use some form of energy to destabilize the neutrino structure. He wants to examine some Phi plasma in orbit. He suggests that you make a reconnaissance flight and take a certain quantity of plasma in the capsule. It's up to you, but let me know what you decide. I have no opinion. I feel as if I no longer have anything. If I am more in favour of your going, it's because we would at least be making some show of progress. Otherwise, we can only envy G.

Snow.

P.S. All I ask is for you to stay outside the cabin. You can call me on the videophone.

I felt a stir of apprehension as I read the letter, and went over it again carefully before tearing it up and throwing the pieces into the disposal unit.

I went through the same terrible charade that I had begun the previous day, and made up a story for Rheya's benefit. She did not notice the deception, and when I told her that I had to make an inspection and suggested that she come with me she was delighted. We stopped at the kitchen for breakfast – Rheya ate very little – and then made for the library.

Before venturing on the mission suggested by Sartorius,

I wanted to glance through the literature dealing with magnetic fields and neutrino structures. I did not yet have any clear idea of how I would set about it, but I had made up my mind to make an independent check on Sartorius's activities. Not that I would prevent Snow and Sartorius from 'liberating themselves' when the annihilator was completed: I meant to take Rheya out of the Station and wait for the conclusion of the operation in the cabin of an aircraft. I set to work with the automatic librarian. Sometimes it answered my queries by ejecting a card with the laconic inscription 'Not on file,' sometimes it practically submerged me under such a spate of specialist physics textbooks that I hesitated to use its advice. Yet I had no desire to leave the big circular chamber. I felt at ease in my egg, among the rows of cabinets crammed with tape and microfilm. Situated right at the centre of the Station, the library had no windows: It was the most isolated area in the great steel shell, and made me feel relaxed in spite of finding my researches held up.

Wandering across the vast room, I stopped at a set of shelves as high as the ceiling, and holding about 600 volumes – all classics on the history of Solaris, starting with the nine volumes of Giese's monumental and already relatively obsolescent monograph. Display for its own sake was improbable in these surroundings. The collection was a respectful tribute to the memory of the pioneers. I took down the massive volumes of Giese and sat leafing through them. Rheya had also located some reading matter. Looking over her shoulder, I saw that she had picked one of the many books brought out by the first expedition, the *Interplanetary Cookery Book*, which could have been the personal property of Giese himself. She was poring over the recipes adapted to the arduous conditions of interstellar flight. I said nothing, and returned to the book resting on my knees. *Solaris – Ten Years of Exploration* had appeared as volumes 4–12 of the Solariana collection whose most recent additions were numbered in the thousands.

Giese was an unemotional man, but then in the study of Solaris emotion is a hindrance to the explorer. Imagination and premature theorizing are positive disadvantages in approaching a planet where – as has become clear – anything is possible. It is almost certain that the unlikely descriptions of the 'plasmatic' metamorphoses of the ocean are faithful accounts of the phenomena observed, although these descriptions are unverifiable, since the ocean seldom repeats itself. The freakish character and gigantic scale of these phenomena go too far outside the experience of man to be grasped by anybody observing them for the first time, and who would consider analogous occurrences as 'sports of nature,' accidental manifestations of blind forces, if he saw them on a reduced scale, say in a mud-volcano on Earth.

Genius and mediocrity alike are dumbfounded by the teeming diversity of the oceanic formations of Solaris; no man has ever become genuinely conversant with them. Giese was by no means a mediocrity, but nor was he a genius. He was a scholarly classifier, the type whose compulsive application to their work utterly divorces them from the pressures of everyday life. Giese devised a plain descriptive terminology, supplemented by terms of his own invention, and although these were inadequate, and sometimes clumsy, it has to be admitted that no semantic system is as yet available to illustrate the behaviour of the ocean. The 'tree-mountains', 'extensors', 'fungoids', 'mimoids', 'symmetriads' and 'asymmetriads', 'vertebrids' and 'agilus' are artificial, linguistically awkward terms, but they do give some impression of Solaris to anyone who has only seen the planet in blurred photographs and incomplete films. The fact is that in spite of his cautious nature the scrupulous Giese more than once jumped to premature conclusions. Even when on their guard, human beings inevitably theorize. Giese, who thought himself immune to temptation, decided that the 'extensors' came into the category of basic forms. He compared them to accumulations of gigantic waves, similar to the tidal movements of our Terran oceans. In the first edition of his work, we find them originally named as 'tides'. This geocentrism might be considered amusing if it did not underline the dilemma in which he found himself.

As soon as the question of comparisons with Earth arises, it must be understood that the 'extensors' are formations that dwarf the Grand Canyon, that they are produced in a substance which externally resembles a yeasty colloid (during this fantastic 'fermentation', the yeast sets into festoons of starched open-work lace; some experts refer to 'ossified tumours'), and that deeper down the substance becomes increasingly resistant, like a tensed muscle which fifty feet below the surface is as hard as rock but retains its flexibility. The 'extensor' appears to be an independent creation, stretching for miles between membranous walls swollen with 'ossified growths', like some colossal python which after swallowing a mountain is sluggishly digesting the meal, while a slow shudder occasionally ripples along its creeping body. The 'extensor' only looks like a lethargic reptile from overhead. At close quarters, when the two 'canyon walls' loom hundreds of yards above the exploring aircraft, it can be seen that this inflated cylinder, reaching from one side of the horizon to the other, is bewilderingly alive with movement. First you notice the continual rotating motion of a greyish-green, oily sludge which reflects blinding sunlight, but skimming just above the 'back of the python' (the 'ravine' sheltering the 'extensor' now resembles the sides of a geological fault), you realize that the motion is in fact far more complex, and consists of concentric fluctuations traversed by darker currents. Occasionally this mantle turns into a shining crust that reflects sky and clouds and then is riddled by explosive eruptions of the internal gases and fluids. The observer slowly realizes that he is looking at the guiding forces that are thrusting outward and upward the two gradually crystallizing gelatinous walls. Science does not accept the obvious without further proof, however, and virulent controversies have reverberated down the years on the key question of the exact sequence of events in the interior of the 'extensors' that furrow the vast living ocean in their millions.

Various organic functions have been ascribed to the 'extensors'. Some experts have argued that their purpose is the transformation of matter; others suggested respiratory processes; still others claimed that they conveyed alimentary materials. An infinite variety of hypotheses now moulder in library basements, eliminated by ingenious, sometimes dangerous experiments. Today, the scientists will go no further than to refer to the 'extensors' as relatively simple, stable formations whose duration is measurable in weeks – an exceptional characteristic among the recorded phenomena of the planet.

The 'mimoid' formations are considerably more complex and bizarre, and elicit a more vehement response from the observer, an instinctive response, I mean. It can be stated without exaggeration that Giese fell in love with the 'mimoids' and was soon devoting all his time to them. For the rest of his life, he studied and described them and brought all his ingenuity to bear on defining their nature. The name he gave them indicates their most astonishing characteristic, the imitation of objects, near or far, external to the ocean itself.

Concealed at first beneath the ocean surface, a large flattened disc appears, ragged, with a tar-like coating. After a few hours, it begins to separate into flat sheets which rise slowly. The observer now becomes a spectator at what looks like a fight to the death as massed ranks of waves converge from all directions like contorted, fleshy mouths which snap greedily around the tattered, fluttering leaf, then plunge into the depths. As each ring of waves breaks and sinks, the fall of this mass of hundreds of thousands of tons is accompanied for an instant by a viscous rumbling, an immense thunderclap. The tarry leaf is overwhelmed, battered and torn apart;

with every fresh assault, circular fragments scatter and drift like feebly fluttering wings below the ocean surface. They bunch into pear-shaped clusters or long strings, merge and rise again, and drag with them an undertow of coagulated shreds of the base of the primal disc. The encircling waves continue to break around the steadily expanding crater. This phenomenon may persist for a day or linger on for a month, and sometimes there are no further developments. The conscientious Giese dubbed this first variation a 'stillbirth', convinced that each of these upheavals aspired towards an ultimate condition, the 'major mimoid', like a polyp colony (only covering an area greater than a town) of pale outcroppings with the faculty of imitating foreign bodies. Uyvens, on the other hand, saw this final stage as constituting a degeneration or necrosis: according to him, the appearance of the 'copies' corresponded to a localized dissipation of the life energies of the ocean, which was no longer in control of the original forms it created.

Giese would not abandon his account of the various phases of the process as a sustained progression towards perfection, with a conviction which is particularly surprising coming from a man of such a moderate, cautious turn of mind in advancing the most trivial hypothesis on the other creations of the ocean. Normally he had all the boldness of an ant crawling up a glacier.

Viewed from above, the mimoid resembles a town, an illusion produced by our compulsion to superimpose analogies with what we know. When the sky is clear, a shimmering heat-haze covers the pliant structures of the clustered polyps surmounted by membranous palisades. The first cloud passing overhead wakens the mimoid. All the outcrops suddenly sprout new shoots, then the mass of polyps ejects a thick tegument which dilates, puffs out, changes colour and in the space of a few minutes has produced an astonishing imitation of the volutes of a cloud. The enormous 'object' casts a reddish shadow over the mimoid, whose peaks ripple and bend together, always in the opposite direction to the movement of the real cloud. I imagine that Giese would have been ready to give his right hand to discover what made the mimoids behave in this way, but these 'isolated' productions are nothing in comparison to the frantic activity the mimoid displays when 'stimulated' by objects of human origin.

The reproduction process embraces every object inside a radius of eight or nine miles. Usually the facsimile is an enlargement of the original, whose forms are sometimes only roughly copied. The reproduction of machines, in particular, elicits simplifications that might be considered grotesque – practically caricatures. The copy is always modelled in the same colourless tegument, which hovers above the outcrops, linked to its base by flimsy umbilical cords; it slides, creeps, curls back on itself, shrinks or swells and finally assumes the most complicated forms. An aircraft, a net or a pole are all reproduced at the same speed. The mimoid is not stimulated by human beings themselves, and in fact it does not react to any living matter, and has never copied, for example, the plants imported for experimental purposes. On the other hand, it will readily reproduce a puppet or a doll, a carving of a dog, or a tree sculpted in any material.

The observer must bear in mind that the 'obedience' of the mimoid does not constitute evidence of cooperation, since it is not consistent. The most highly evolved mimoid has its off-days, when it 'lives' in slow-motion, or its pulsation weakens. (This pulsation is invisible to the naked eye, and was only discovered after close examination of rapid-motion film of the mimoid, which revealed that each 'beat' took two hours.)

During these 'off-days,' it is easy to explore the mimoid, especially if it is old, for the base anchored in the ocean, like the protuberances growing out of it, is relatively solid, and provides a firm footing for a man. It is equally possible to remain inside the mimoid during periods of activity, except that visibility is close to nil because of the whitish colloidal dust continually emitted through tears in the tegument above. In any case, at close range it is impossible to distinguish what forms the tegument is assuming, on account of their vast size – the smallest 'copy' is the size of a mountain. In addition, a thick layer of colloidal snow quickly covers the base of the mimoid: this spongy carpet takes several hours to solidify (the 'frozen' crust will take the weight of a man, though its composition is much lighter than pumice stone). The problem is that without special equipment there is a risk of being lost in the maze of tangled structures and crevasses, sometimes reminiscent of jumbled colonnades, sometimes of petrified geysers. Even in daylight it is easy to lose one's direction, for the sun's rays cannot pierce the white ceiling ejected into the atmosphere by the 'imitative explosions'.

On gala days (for the scientist as well as for the mimoid), an unforgettable spectacle develops as the mimoid goes into hyperproduction and performs wild flights of fancy. It plays variations on the theme of a given object and embroiders 'formal extensions' that amuse it for hours on end, to the delight of the non-figurative artist and the despair of the scientist, who is at a loss to grasp any common theme in the performance. The mimoid can produce 'primitive' simplifications, but is just as likely to indulge in 'baroque' deviations, paroxysms of extravagant brilliance. Old mimoids tend to manufacture extremely comic forms. Looking at the photographs, I have never been moved to laughter; the riddle they set is too disquieting to be funny.

During the early years of exploration, the scientists literally threw themselves upon the mimoids, which were spoken of as open windows on the ocean and the best opportunity to establish the hoped-for contact between the two civilizations. They were soon forced to admit that there was not the slightest prospect of communication, and that the entire process began and ended with the reproduction of forms. The mimoids were a dead end.

Giving way to the temptations of a latent anthropomorphism or zoomorphism, there were many schools of thought which saw various other oceanic formations as 'sensory organs', even as 'limbs', which was how experts like Maartens and Ekkonai classified Giese's 'vertebrids' and 'agilus' for a time. Anyone who is rash enough to see protuberances that reach as far as two miles into the atmosphere as limbs might just as well claim that earthquakes are the gymnastics of the Earth's crust!

Three hundred chapters of Giese catalogue the standard formations which occur on the surface of the living ocean and which can be seen in dozens, even hundreds, in the course of any day. The symmetriads – to continue using the terminology and definitions of the Giese school – are the least 'human' formations, which is to say that they bear no resemblance whatsoever to anything on Earth. By the time the symmetriads were being investigated, it was already clear that the ocean was not aggressive, and that its plasmatic eddies would not swallow any but the most foolhardy explorer (of course I am not including accidents resulting from mechanical failures). It is possible to fly in complete safety from one part to another of the cylindrical body of an extensor, or of the vertebrids, Jacob's ladders oscillating among the clouds: the plasma retreats at the speed of sound in the planet's atmosphere to make way for any foreign body. Deep funnels will open even beneath the surface of the ocean (at a prodigious expenditure of energy, calculated by Scriabin at around 10^{19} ergs). Nevertheless, the first venture into the interior of a symmetriad was undertaken with the utmost caution and discipline, and involved a host of what turned out to be unnecessary safety measures. Every schoolboy on Earth knows the names of these pioneers.

It is not their nightmare appearance that makes the gigantic symmetriad formations dangerous, but the total instability and capriciousness of their structure, in which even the laws of physics do not hold. The theory that the living ocean is endowed with intelligence has found its firmest adherents among those scientists who have ventured into their unpredictable depths.

The birth of a symmetriad comes like a sudden eruption. About an hour beforehand, an area of tens of square miles of ocean vitrifies and begins to shine. It remains fluid, and there is no alteration in the rhythm of the waves. Occasionally the phenomenon of vitrification occurs in the neighbourhood of the funnel left by an agilus. The gleaming sheath of the ocean heaves upwards to form a vast ball that reflects sky, sun, clouds and the entire horizon in a medley of changing, variegated images. Diffracted light creates a kaleidoscopic play of colour.

The effects of light on a symmetriad are especially striking during the blue day and the red sunset. The planet appears to be giving birth to a twin that increases in volume from one moment to the next. The immense flaming globe has scarcely reached its maximum expansion above the ocean when it bursts at the summit and cracks vertically. It is not breaking up; this is the second phase, which goes under the clumsy name of the 'floral calyx phase' and lasts only a few seconds. The membranous arches soaring into the sky now fold inwards and merge to produce a thickset trunk enclosing a scene of teeming activity. At the centre of the trunk, which was explored for the first time by the seventy-man Hamalei expedition, a process of polycrystallization on a giant scale erects an axis commonly referred to as the 'backbone,' a term which I consider ill-chosen. The mind-bending architecture of this central pillar is held in place by vertical shafts of a gelatinous, almost liquid consistency, constantly gushing upwards out of wide crevasses. Meanwhile, the entire trunk is surrounded by a belt of snowy foam, seething with great bubbles of gas, and the whole process is accompanied by a perpetual dull roar of sound. From the centre towards the periphery, powerful buttresses spin out and are coated with streams of ductile matter rising out of the ocean depths.

Simultaneously the gelatinous geysers are converted into mobile columns that proceed to extrude tendrils that reach out in clusters towards points rigorously predetermined by the overall dynamics of the entire structure: they call to mind the gills of an embryo, except that they are revolving at fantastic speed and ooze trickles of pinkish 'blood' and a dark green secretion.

The symmetriad now begins to display its most exotic characteristic – the property of 'illustrating', sometimes contradicting, various laws of physics. (Bear in mind that no two symmetriads are alike, and that the geometry of each one is a unique 'invention' of the living ocean.) The interior of the symmetriad becomes a factory for the production of 'monumental machines', as these constructs are sometimes called, although they resemble no machine which it is within the power of mankind to build: the designation is applied because all this activity has finite ends, and is therefore in some sense 'mechanical'.

When the geysers of oceanic matter have solidified into pillars or into three-dimensional networks of galleries and passages, and the 'membranes' are set into an inextricable pattern of storeys, panels and vaults, the symmetriad justifies its name, for the entire structure is divided into two segments each mirroring the other to the most infinitesimal detail.

After twenty or thirty minutes, when the axis may have tilted as much as eight to ten degrees from the horizontal, the giant begins slowly to subside. (Symmetriads vary in size, but as the base begins to submerge even the smallest reach a height of half a mile, and are visible from miles away.) At last, the structure stabilizes itself, and the partly submerged symmetriad ceases its activity. It is now possible to explore it in complete safety by making an entry near the summit, through one of the many syphons which emerge from the dome. The completed symmetriad represents a spatial analogue of some transcendental equation.

It is a commonplace that any equation can be expressed in

the figurative language of non-Euclidean geometry and represented in three dimensions. This interpretation relates the symmetriad to Lobachevsky's cones and Riemann's negative curves, although its unimaginable complexity makes the relationship highly tenuous. The eventual form occupies an area of several cubic miles and extends far beyond our whole system of mathematics. In addition, this extension is four-dimensional, for the fundamental terms of the equations use a temporal symbolism expressed in the internal changes over a given period.

It would be only natural, clearly, to suppose that the symmetriad is a 'computer' of the living ocean, performing calculations for a purpose that we are not able to grasp. This was Fremont's theory, now generally discounted. The hypothesis was a tempting one, but it proved impossible to sustain the concept that the living ocean examined problems of matter, the cosmos and existence through the medium of titanic eruptions, in which every particle had an indispensable function as a controlled element in an analytical system of infinite purity. In fact, numerous phenomena contradict this over-simplified (some say childishly naïve) concept.

Any number of attempts have been made to transpose and 'illustrate' the symmetriad, and Averian's demonstration was particularly well received. Let us imagine, he said, an edifice dating from the great days of Babylon, but built of some living, sensitive substance with the capacity to evolve: the architectonics of this edifice passes through a series of phases, and we see it adopt the forms of a Greek, then of a Roman building. The columns sprout like branches and become narrower, the roof grows lighter, rises, curves, the arch describes an abrupt parabola then breaks down into an arrow shape: the Gothic is born, comes to maturity and gives way in time to new forms. Austerity of line gives way to a riot of exploding lines and shapes, and the baroque runs wild. If the progression continues – and the successive mutations are to be seen as stages in the life of an evolving organism – we finally arrive at the architecture of the space age, and perhaps too at some understanding of the symmetriad.

Unfortunately, no matter how this demonstration may be expanded and improved (there have been attempts to visualize it with the aid of models and films), the comparison remains superficial. It is evasive and illusory, and side-steps the central fact that the symmetriad is quite unlike anything Earth has ever produced.

The human mind is only capable of absorbing a few things at a time. We see what is taking place in front of us in the here and now, and cannot envisage simultaneously a succession of processes, no matter how integrated and complementary. Our faculties of perception are consequently limited even as regards fairly simple phenomena. The fate of a single man can be rich with significance, that of a few hundred less so, but the history of thousands and millions of men does not mean anything at all, in any adequate sense of the word. The symmetriad is a million – a billion, rather – raised to the power of N: it is incomprehensible. We pass through vast halls, each with a capacity of ten Kronecker units, and creep like so many ants clinging to the folds of breathing vaults and craning to watch the flight of soaring girders, opalescent in the glare of searchlights, and elastic domes which criss-cross and balance each other unerringly, the perfection of a moment, since everything here passes and fades. The essence of this architecture is movement synchronized towards a precise objective. We observe a fraction of the process, like hearing the vibration of a single string in an orchestra of supergiants. We know, but cannot grasp, that above and below, beyond the limits of perception or imagination, thousands and millions of simultaneous transformations are at work, interlinked like a musical score by mathematical counterpoint. It has been described as a symphony in geometry, but we lack the ears to hear it.

Only a long-distance view would reveal the entire process,

but the outer covering of the symmetriad conceals the colossal inner matrix where creation is unceasing, the created becomes the creator, and absolutely identical 'twins' are born at opposite poles, separated by towering structures and miles of distance. The symphony creates itself, and writes its own conclusion, which is terrible to watch. Every observer feels like a spectator at a tragedy or a public massacre, when after two or three hours – never longer – the living ocean stages its assault. The polished surface of the ocean swirls and crumples, the desiccated foam liquefies again, begins to seethe, and legions of waves pour inwards from every point of the horizon, their gaping mouths far more massive than the greedy lips that surround the embryonic mimoid. The submerged base of the symmetriad is compressed, and the colossus rises as if on the point of being shot out of the planet's gravitational pull. The upper layers of the ocean redouble their activity, and the waves surge higher and higher to lick against the sides of the symmetriad. They envelop it, harden and plug the orifices, but their attack is nothing compared to the scene in the interior. First the process of creation freezes momentarily; then there is 'panic'. The smooth interpenetration of moving forms and the harmonious play of planes and lines accelerates, and the impression is inescapable that the symmetriad is hurrying to complete some task in the face of danger. The awe inspired by the metamorphosis and dynamics of the symmetriad intensifies as the proud sweep of the domes falters, vaults sag and droop, and 'wrong notes' – incomplete, mangled forms – make their appearance. A powerful moaning roar issues from the invisible depths like a sigh of agony, reverberates through the narrow funnels and booms through the collapsing domes. In spite of the growing destructive violence of these convulsions, the spectator is rooted to the spot. Only the force of the hurricane streaming out of the depths and howling through the thousands of galleries keeps the great structure erect. Soon it subsides and starts to disintegrate. There are final flutterings, contortions, and blind, random spasms. Gnawed and undermined, the giant sinks slowly and disappears, and the space where it stood is covered with whirlpools of foam.

So what does all this mean?

I remembered an incident dating from my spell as assistant to Gibarian. A group of schoolchildren visiting the Solarist Institute in Aden were making their way through the main hall of the library and looking at the racks of microfilm that occupied the entire left-hand side of the hall. The guide explained that among other phenomena immortalized by the image, these contained fragmentary glimpses of symmetriads long since vanished – not single shots, but whole reels, more than ninety thousand of them!

One plump schoolgirl (she looked about fifteen, peering inquisitively over her spectacles) abruptly asked: 'And what is it for?'

In the ensuing embarrassed silence, the schoolmistress was content to dart a reproving look at her wayward pupil. Among the Solarists whose job was to act as guides (I was one of them), no one would produce an answer. Each symmetriad is unique, and the developments in its heart are, generally speaking, unpredictable. Sometimes there is no sound. Sometimes the index of refraction increases or diminishes. Sometimes rhythmic pulsations are accompanied by local changes in gravitation, as if the heart of the symmetriad were beating by gravitating. Sometimes the compasses of the observers spin wildly, and ionized layers spring up and disappear. The catalogue could go on indefinitely. In any case, even if we did ever succeed in solving the riddle of the symmetriads, we would still have to contend with the asymmetriads!

The asymmetriads are born in the same manner as the symmetriads but finish differently, and nothing can be seen of their internal processes except tremors, vibrations and flickering. We do know, however, that the interior houses bewildering operations performed at a speed that defies the laws of physics and which are dubbed 'giant quantic phenomena'. The mathematical analogy with certain three-dimensional models of the atom is so unstable and transitory that some commentators dismiss the resemblance as of secondary importance, if not purely accidental. The asymmetriads have a very short life-span of fifteen to twenty minutes, and their death is even more appalling than that of the symmetriads: with the howling gale that screams through its fabric, a thick fluid gushes out, gurgles hideously, and submerges everything beneath a foul, bubbling foam. Then an explosion, coinciding with a muddy eruption, hurls up a spout of debris which rains slowly down into the seething ocean. This debris is sometimes found scores of miles from the focus of the explosion, dried up, yellow and flattened, like flakes of cartilage.

Some other creations of the ocean, which are much more rare and of very variable duration, part company with the parent body entirely. The first traces of these 'independents' were identified – wrongly, it was later proved – as the remains of creatures inhabiting the ocean deeps. The free-ranging forms are often reminiscent of many-winged birds, darting away from the moving trunks of the agilus, but the preconceptions of Earth offer no assistance in unravelling the mysteries of Solaris. Strange, seal-like bodies appear now and then on the rocky outcrop of an island, sprawling in the sun or dragging themselves lazily back to merge with the ocean.

There was no escaping the impressions that grew out of man's experience on Earth. The prospects of Contact receded.

Explorers travelled hundreds of miles in the depths of symmetriads, and installed measuring instruments and remote-control cameras. Artificial satellites captured the birth of mimoids and extensors, and faithfully reproduced their images of growth and destruction. The libraries overflowed, the archives grew, and the price paid for all this documentation was often very heavy. One notorious disaster cost 106 people their lives, among them Giese himself: while studying what was undoubtedly a symmetriad, the expedition was suddenly destroyed by a process peculiar to the asymmetriads. In two seconds, an eruption of glutinous mud swallowed up seventy-nine men and all their equipment. Another twenty-seven observers surveying the area from aircraft and helicopters were also caught in the eruption.

Following the Eruption of the 106, and for the first time in Solarist studies, there were petitions demanding a thermonuclear attack on the ocean. Such a response would have been more cruelty than revenge, since it would have meant destroying what we did not understand. Tsanken's ultimatum, which was never officially acknowledged, probably influenced the negative outcome of the vote. He was in command of Giese's reserve team, and had survived owing to a transmission error that took him off his course, to arrive in the disaster area a few minutes after the explosion, when the black mushroom cloud was still visible. Informed of the proposal for a nuclear strike, he threatened to blow up the Station, together with the nineteen survivors sheltering inside it.

Today, there are only three of us in the Station. Its construction was controlled by satellites, and was a technical feat on which the human race has a right to pride itself, even if the ocean builds far more impressive structures in the space of a few seconds. The Station is a disc of 100 yards radius, and contains four decks at the centre and two at the circumference. It is maintained at a height of from 500 to 1500 yards above the ocean by gravitors programmed to compensate for the ocean's own field of attraction. In addition to all the machines available to ordinary Stations and the large artificial satellites that orbit other planets, the Solaris Station is equipped with specialized radar apparatus sensitive to the smallest fluctuations of the ocean surface, which trips auxiliary power-circuits capable of thrusting the steel disc into the stratosphere at the first indication of new plasmatic upheavals.

But today, in spite of the presence of our faithful 'visitors', the Station was strangely deserted. Ever since the robots had been locked away in the lower-deck store-rooms – for a reason I had still not discovered – it had been possible to walk around without meeting a single member of the crew of our ghost ship.

As I replaced the ninth volume of Giese on the shelf, the plastic-coated steel floor seemed to shudder under my feet. I stood still, but the vibration had stopped. The library was completely isolated from the other rooms, and the only possible source of vibration must be a shuttle leaving the Station. This thought jerked me back to reality. I had not yet decided to accept Sartorius's suggestion and leave the Station. By feigning approval of his plan, I had been more or less postponing the outbreak of hostilities, for I was determined to save Rheya. All the same, Sartorius might have some chance of success. He certainly had the advantage of being a qualified physicist, while I was in the ironic position of having to count on the superiority of the ocean. I pored over microfilm texts for an hour, and made myself wrestle with the unfamiliar language of neutrino physics. The undertaking seemed hopeless at first: there were no less than five current theories dealing with neutrino fields, an obvious indication that none was definitive. Eventually I struck promising ground, and was busily copying down equations when there was a knock at the door. I got up quickly and opened it a few inches, to see Snow's perspiring face, and behind him an empty corridor.

'Yes, it's me.' His voice was hoarse, and there were dark pouches under the bloodshot eyes. He wore an anti-radiation apron of shiny rubber, and the same worn old trousers held up by elastic braces.

Snow's gaze flickered round the circular chamber and

alighted on Rheya where she stood by an armchair at the other end. Then it returned to me, and I lowered my eyelids imperceptibly. He nodded, and I spoke casually:

'Rheya, come and meet Dr Snow . . . Snow – my wife.'

'I . . . I'm just a minor member of the crew. Don't get about much . . .' He faltered, but managed to blurt out: 'That's why I haven't had the pleasure of meeting you before . . .'

Rheya smiled and held out her hand, which he shook in some surprise. He blinked several times and stood looking at her, tongue-tied, until I took him by the arm.

'Excuse me,' he said to Rheya. 'I wanted a word with you, Kelvin . . .'

'Of course.' (My composure was an ugly charade, but what else could I do?) 'Take no notice of us, Rheya. We'll be talking shop . . .'

I guided Snow over to the chairs on the far side of the room, and Rheya sat in the armchair I had occupied earlier, swivelling it so that she could glance up at us from her book. I lowered my voice:

'Any news?'

'I'm divorced,' he whispered. If anybody had quoted this to me as the opening of a conversation a few days before, I would have burst out laughing, but the Station had blunted my sense of humour. 'It feels like years since yesterday morning,' he went on. 'And you?'

'Nothing.' I was at a loss for words. I liked Snow, but I distrusted him, or rather I distrusted the purpose of his visit.

'Nothing? Surely . . .'

'What?' I pretended not to understand.

Eyes half shut, he leant so close to me that I could feel his breath on my face:

'This business has all of us confused, Kelvin. I can't make contact with Sartorius. All I know is what I wrote to you, which is what he told me after our little conference . . .'

'Has he disconnected his videophone?'

'No, there's been a short-circuit at his end. He could have

done it on purpose, but there's also . . .' He clenched his fist and mimed somebody aiming a punch, curling his lips in an unpleasant grin. 'Kelvin, I came here to . . . What do you intend doing?'

'You want my answer to your letter. All right, I'll go on the trip, there's no reason for me to refuse. I've only been getting ready . . .'

'No,' he interrupted. 'It isn't that.'

'What then? Go on.'

'Sartorius thinks he may be on the right track,' Snow muttered. His eyes never left me, and I had to stay still and try to look casual. 'It all started with that X-ray experiment that he and Gibarian arranged, you remember. That could have produced some alteration . . .'

'What kind of alteration?'

'They beamed the rays directly into the ocean. The intensity was only modulated according to a pre-set program.'

'I know. It's already been done by Nilin and a lot of others.'

'Yes, but the others worked on low power. This time they used everything we had.'

'That could lead to trouble . . . violating the four-power convention, and the United Nations . . . '

'Come on, Kelvin, you know as well as I do that it doesn't matter now. Gibarian is dead.'

'So Sartorius makes him the scapegoat?'

'I don't know. We haven't talked about that. Sartorius is intrigued by the visiting hours. They only come as we wake up, which suggests that the ocean is especially interested in our sleeping hours, and that that is when it locates its patterns. Sartorius wants to send our waking selves – our conscious thoughts. You see?'

'By mail?'

'Keep the jokes to yourself. The idea is to modulate the X-rays by hooking in an electro-encephalograph taken from one of us.'

133

'Ah!' Light was beginning to dawn. 'And that one of us is me?'

'Yes, Sartorius had you in mind.'

'Tell him I'm flattered.'

'Will you do it?'

I hesitated. Snow darted a look at Rheya, who seemed absorbed in her book. I felt my face turn pale.

'Well?'

'The idea of using X-rays to preach sermons on the greatness of mankind seems absolutely ridiculous to me. Don't you think so?'

'You mean it?'

'Yes.'

'Right,' he said, smiling as if I had fallen in with some idea of his own, 'then you're opposed to the plan?'

His expression told me that he had somehow been a step ahead of me all the time.

'Okay,' he went on. 'There is a second plan – to construct a Roche apparatus.'

'An annihilator?'

'Yes. Sartorius has already made the preliminary calculations. It is feasible, and it won't even require any great expenditure of energy. The apparatus will generate a negative field twenty-four hours a day, and for an unlimited period.'

'And its effect?'

'Simple. It will be a negative neutrino field. Ordinary matter will not be affected at all. Only the . . . neutrino structures will be destroyed. You see?'

Snow gave me a satisfied grin. I stood stock-still and gaping, so that he stopped smiling, looked at me with a frown, and waited a moment before speaking:

'We abandon the first plan then, the "Brainwave" plan? Sartorius is working on the other one right now. We'll call it "Project Liberation".'

I had to make a quick decision. Snow was no physicist,

and Sartorius's videophone was disconnected or smashed. I took the chance:

'I'd rather call the second idea "Operation Slaughterhouse".'

'And you ought to know! Don't tell me you haven't had some practice lately. Only there'll be a radical difference this time – no more visitors, no more Phi-creatures – they will disintegrate as soon as they appear.'

I nodded, and managed what I hoped was a convincing smile:

'You haven't got the point. Morality is one thing, but self-preservation ... I just don't want to get us all killed, Snow.'

He stared back at me suspiciously, as I showed him my scribbled equations:

'I've been working along the same lines. Don't look so surprised. The neutrino theory was my idea in the first place, remember? Look. Negative fields can be generated all right. And ordinary matter is unaffected. But what happens to the energy that maintains the neutrino structure when it disintegrates? There must be a considerable release of that energy. Assuming a kilogram of ordinary matter represents 10^8 ergs, for a Phi-creation we get 5^7 multiplied by 10^8. That means the equivalent of a small atomic bomb exploding inside the Station.'

'You mean to tell me Sartorius won't have been over all this?'

It was my turn to grin maliciously:

'Not necessarily. Sartorius follows the Frazer–Cajolla school. Their theories would indicate that the energy potential would be given off in the form of light – powerful, yes, but not destructive. But that isn't the only theory of neutrino fields. According to Cayatte, and Avalov, and Sion, the radiation-spectrum would be much broader. At its maximum, there would be a strong burst of gamma radiation. Sartorius has faith in his tutors. I don't say we can't respect that, but there are other tutors, and other theories. And another thing, Snow' – I could see him beginning to waver – 'we have to bear in mind the ocean itself! It is bound to have used the optimum means of designing its creations. It seems to me that we can't afford to back Sartorius against the ocean as well as the other theories.'

'Give me that paper, Kelvin.'

I passed it to him, and he pored over my equations. 'What's this?' He pointed to a line of calculations.

'That? The transformation tensor of the magnetic field.'

'Give it here.'

'Why?' (I already knew his reply.)

'I'll have to show Sartorius.'

'If you say so.' I shrugged. 'You're welcome to it, naturally, provided you realize that these theories have never been tested experimentally: neutrino structures have been abstractions until now. Sartorius is relying on Frazer, and I've followed Sion's theory. He'll say I'm no physicist, or Sion either, not from his point of view, at least. He will dispute my figures, and I'm not going to get into the kind of argument where he tries to browbeat me for his own satisfaction. You, I can convince. I couldn't begin to convince Sartorius, and I have no intention of trying.'

'Then what *do* you want to do? He's already started work . . .'

All his earlier animation had subsided, and he spoke in a monotone. I did not know if he trusted me, and I did not much care:

'What do I want to do? Whatever a man does when his life is in danger.'

'I'll try to contact him. Maybe he can develop some kind of safety device . . . And then there's the first plan. Would you cooperate? Sartorius would agree, I'm sure of it. At least it's worth a try.'

'You think so?'

'No,' he snapped back. 'But what have we got to lose?'

I was in no hurry to accept. It was time that I needed, and Snow could help me to prolong the delay:

'I'll think about it.'

'Okay, I'm going.' His bones creaked as he got up. 'We'll have to begin with the encephalogram,' he said, rubbing at his overall as if to get rid of some invisible stain.

Without a word to Rheya, he walked to the door, and after it had closed behind him I got up and crumpled the sheet of paper in my hand. I had not falsified the equations, but I doubted whether Sion would have agreed with my extensions of his theory. I started abruptly, as Rheya's hand touched my shoulder.

'Kris, who is he?'

'I told you, Dr Snow.'

'What's he like?'

'I don't know him very well . . . why?'

'He was giving me such a strange look.'

'So you're an attractive woman . . .'

'No, this was a different sort of look . . . as if . . .' She trembled, looked up at me momentarily, then lowered her eyes. 'Let's go back to the cabin.'

The Liquid Oxygen

I have no idea how long I had been lying in the dark, staring at the luminous dial of my wristwatch. Hearing myself breathing, I felt a vague surprise, but my underlying feeling was one of profound indifference both to this ring of phosphorescent figures and to my own surprise. I told myself that the feeling was caused by fatigue. When I turned over, the bed seemed wider than usual. I held my breath; no sound broke the silence. Rheya's breathing should have been audible. I reached out, but felt nothing. I was alone.

I was about to call her name, when I heard the tread of heavy footsteps coming towards me. A numb calm descended:

'Gibarian?'

'Yes, it's me. Don't switch the light on.'

'No?'

'There's no need, and it's better for us to stay in the dark.'

'But you are dead . . .'

'Don't let that worry you. You recognize my voice, don't you?'

'Yes. Why did you kill yourself?'

'I had no choice. You arrived four days late. If you had come earlier, I would not have been forced to kill myself. Don't worry about it, though, I don't regret anything.'

'You really are there? I'm not asleep?'

'Oh, you think you're dreaming about me? As you did with Rheya?'

'Where is she?'

'How should I know?'

'I have a feeling that you do.'

'Keep your feelings for yourself. Let's say I'm deputizing for her.'

'I want her here too!'

'Not possible.'

'Why not? You know very well that it isn't the real you, just my . . .'

'No, I am the real Gibarian – just a new incarnation. But let's not waste time on useless chatter.'

'You'll be leaving again?'

'Yes.'

'And then she'll come back?'

'Why should you care about that?'

'She belongs to me.'

'You are afraid of her.'

'No.''

'She disgusts you.'

'What do you want with me?'

'Save your pity for yourself – you have a right to it – but not for her. She will always be twenty years old. You must know that.'

I felt suddenly at ease again, for no apparent reason, and ready to hear him out. He seemed to have come closer, though I could not see him in the dark.

'What do you want?'

'Sartorius has convinced Snow that you have been deceiving him. Right now they are trying to give you the same treatment. Building the X-ray beamer is a cover for constructing a magnetic field disruptor.'

'Where is she?'

'Didn't you hear me? I came to warn you.'

'Where is she?'

'I don't know. Be careful. You must find some kind of weapon. You can't trust anyone.'

'I can trust Rheya.'

He stifled a laugh:

'Of course, you can trust Rheya – to some extent. And you can always follow my example, if all else fails.'

'You are not Gibarian.'

'No? Then who am I? A dream?'

'No, you are only a puppet. But you don't realize that you are.'

'And how do you know what *you* are?'

I tried to stand up, but could not stir. Although Gibarian was still speaking, I could not understand his words; there was only the drone of his voice. I struggled to regain control of my body, felt a sudden wrench and . . . I woke up, and drew down great gulps of air. It was dark, and I had been having a nightmare. And now I heard a distant, monotonous voice: '. . . a dilemma that we are not equipped to solve. We are the cause of our own sufferings. The polytheres behave strictly as a kind of amplifier of our own thoughts. Any attempt to understand the motivation of these occurrences is blocked by our own anthropomorphism. Where there are no men, there cannot be motives accessible to men. Before we can proceed with our research, either our own thoughts or their materialized forms must be destroyed. It is not within our power to destroy our thoughts. As for destroying their material forms, that could be like committing murder.'

I had recognized Gibarian's voice at once. When I stretched out my arm, I found myself alone. I had fallen asleep again. This was another dream. I called Gibarian's name, and the voice stopped in mid-sentence. There was the sound of a faint gasp, then a gust of air.

'Well, Gibarian,' I yawned, 'you seem to be following me out of one dream and into the next . . .'

There was a rustling sound from somewhere close, and I called his name again. The bed-springs creaked, and a voice whispered in my ear:

'Kris . . . it's me . . .'

'Rheya? Is it you? What about Gibarian?'

'But . . . you said he was dead, Kris.'

'He can be alive in a dream,' I told her dejectedly, although I was not completely sure that it had been a dream. 'He spoke to me . . . He was here . . .'

My head sank back on to the pillow. Rheya said something, but I was already drifting into sleep.

In the red light of morning, the events of the previous night returned. I had dreamt that I was talking to Gibarian. But afterwards, I could swear that I had heard his voice, although I had no clear recall of what he had said, and it had not been a conversation – more like a speech.

Rheya was splashing about in the bathroom. I looked under the bed, where I had hidden the tape-recorder a few days earlier. It was no longer there.

'Rheya!' She put her face round the door. 'Did you see a tape-recorder under the bed, a little pocket one?'

'There was a pile of stuff under the bed. I put it all over there.' She pointed to a shelf by the medicine cabinet, and disappeared back into the bathroom.

There was no tape-recorder on the shelf, and when Rheya emerged from the bathroom I asked her to think again. She sat combing her hair, and did not answer. It was not until now that I noticed how pale she was, and how closely she was watching me in the mirror. I returned to the attack:

'The tape-recorder is missing, Rheya.'

'Is that all you have to tell me?'

'I'm sorry. You're right, it's silly to get so worked up about a tape-recorder.'

Anything to avoid a quarrel.

Later, over breakfast, the change in Rheya's behaviour was obvious, yet I could not define it. She did not meet my eyes, and was frequently so lost in thought that she did not hear me. Once, when she looked up, her cheeks were damp.

'Is anything the matter? You're crying.'

'Leave me alone,' Rheya blurted. 'They aren't real tears.'

Perhaps I ought not to have let her answer so, but 'straight talking' was the last thing I wanted. In any case, I had other problems on my mind; I had dreamt that Snow and Sartorius were plotting against me, and although I was certain that it had been nothing more than a dream, I was wondering if there was anything in the Station that I might be able to use to defend myself. My thinking had not progressed to the point of deciding what to do with a weapon once I had it. I told Rheya that I had to make an inspection of the store-rooms, and she trailed behind me silently.

I ransacked packing-cases and capsules, and when we reached the lower deck I was unable to resist looking into the cold store. Not wanting Rheya to go in, I put my head inside the door and looked around. The recumbent figure was still covered by its dark shroud, but from my position in the doorway I could not make out whether the black woman was still sleeping by Gibarian's body. I had the impression that she was no longer there.

I wandered from one store-room to another, unable to locate anything that might serve as a weapon, and with a rising feeling of depression. All at once I noticed that Rheya was not with me. Then she reappeared; she had been hanging back in the corridor. In spite of the pain she suffered when she could not see me, she had been trying to keep away. I should have been astonished: instead, I went on acting as if I had been offended – but then, who had offended me? – and sulking like a child.

My head was throbbing, and I rifled the entire contents of the medicine-cabinet without finding so much as an aspirin. I did not want to go back to the sick bay. I did not want to do anything. I had never been in a blacker temper. Rheya tip-toed about the cabin like a shadow. Now and then she went off somewhere. I don't know where, I was paying her no attention; then she would creep back inside.

That afternoon, in the kitchen (we had just eaten, but in fact Rheya had not touched her food, and I had not attempted to persuade her), Rheya got up and came to sit next to me. I felt her hand on my sleeve, and grunted:

142

'What's the matter?'

I had been meaning to go up to the deck above, as the pipes were carrying the sharp crackling sound of high-voltage apparatus in use, but Rheya would have had to come with me. It had been hard enough to justify her presence in the library; among the machinery, there was a chance that Snow might drop some clumsy remark. I gave up the idea of going to investigate.

'Kris,' she whispered, 'what's happening to us?'

I gave an involuntary sigh of frustration with everything that had been happening since the previous night:

'Everything is fine. Why?'

'I want to talk.'

'All right, I'm listening.'

'Not like this.'

'What? You know I have a headache, and that's the least of my worries . . .'

'You're not being fair.'

I forced myself to smile; it must have been a poor imitation:

'Go ahead and talk, darling, please.'

'Will you tell me the truth?'

'Why should I lie?' This was an ominous beginning.

'You might have your reasons . . . it might be necessary . . . But if you want . . . Look, I am going to tell you something, and then it will be your turn – only no half-truths. Promise!' I could not meet her gaze. 'I've already told you that I don't know how I came to be here. Perhaps you do. Wait! – perhaps you don't. But if you do know, and you can't tell me now, will you tell me one day, later on? I couldn't be any the worse for it, and you would at least be giving me a chance.'

'What are you talking about, child,' I stammered. 'What chance?'

'Kris, whatever I may be, I'm certainly not a child. You promised me an answer.'

Whatever I may be . . . my throat tightened, and I stared at

143

Rheya shaking my head like an imbecile, as if forbidding myself to hear any more.

'I'm not asking for explanations. You only need to tell me that you are not allowed to say.'

'I'm not hiding anything,' I croaked.

'All right.'

She stood up. I wanted to say something. We could not leave it at that. But no words would come.

'Rheya . . .'

She was standing at the window, with her back turned. The blue-black ocean stretched out under a cloudless sky.

'Rheya, if you believe . . . You know very well I love you . . .'

'Me?'

I went to put my arms round her, but she pulled away.

'You're too kind,' she said. 'You say you love me? I'd rather you beat me.'

'Rheya, darling!'

'No, no, don't say any more.'

She went back to the table and began to clear away the plates. I gazed out at the ocean. The sun was setting, and the Station cast a lengthening shadow that danced on the waves. Rheya dropped a plate on the floor. Water splashed in the sink. A tarnished golden halo ringed the horizon. If I only knew what to do . . . if only . . . Suddenly there was silence. Rheya was standing behind me.

'No, don't turn round,' she murmured. 'It isn't your fault, I know. Don't torment yourself.'

I reached out, but she slipped away to the far side of the room and picked up a stack of plates: 'It's a shame they're unbreakable. I'd like to smash them, all of them.'

I thought for a moment that she really was going to dash them to the floor, but she looked across at me and smiled:

'Don't worry, I'm not going to make scenes.'

In the middle of the night, I was suddenly wide awake. The room was in darkness and the door was ajar, with a faint

144

light shining from the corridor. There was a shrill hissing noise, interspersed with heavy, muffled thudding, as if some heavy object was pounding against a wall. A meteor had pierced the shell of the Station! No, not a meteor, a shuttle, for I could hear a dreadful laboured whining . . .

I shook myself. It was not a meteor, nor was it a shuttle. The sound was coming from somebody at the end of the corridor. I ran down to where light was pouring from the door of the little work-room, and rushed inside. A freezing vapour filled the room, my breath fell like snow, and white flakes swirled over a body covered by a dressing-gown, stirring feebly then striking the floor again. I could hardly see through the freezing mist. I snatched her up and folded her in my arms, and the dressing-gown burnt my skin. Rheya kept on making the same harsh gasping sound as I stumbled along the corridor, no longer feeling the cold, only her breath on my neck, burning like fire.

I lowered Rheya on to the operating-table and pulled the dressing-gown open. Her face was contorted with pain, the lips covered by a thick, black layer of frozen blood, the tongue a mass of sparkling ice crystals.

Liquid oxygen . . . The Dewar bottles in the work-room contained liquid oxygen. Splinters of glass had crunched underfoot as I carried Rheya out. How much of it had she swallowed? It didn't matter. Her trachea, throat and lungs must be burnt away – liquid oxygen corrodes flesh more effectively than strong acids. Her breathing was more and more laboured, with a dry sound like tearing paper. Her eyes were closed. She was dying.

I looked across at the big, glass-fronted cabinets, crammed with instruments and drugs. Tracheotomy? Intubation? She had no lungs! I stared at shelves full of coloured bottles and cartons. She went on gasping hoarsely, and a wisp of vapour drifted out of her open mouth.

Thermophores . . .

I started looking for them, then changed my mind, ran to

another cupboard and turned out boxes of ampoules. Now a hypodermic – where are they? – here – needs sterilizing. I fumbled with the lid of the sterilizer, but my numb fingers had lost all sensation and would not bend.

The harsh rattle grew louder, and Rheya's eyes were open when I reached the table. I opened my mouth to say her name but my voice had gone and my lips would not obey me. My face did not belong to me; it was a plaster mask.

Rheya's ribs were heaving under the white skin. The ice-crystals had melted and her wet hair was entangled in the headrest. And she was looking at me.

'Rheya!' It was all I could say. I stood paralysed, my hands dangling uselessly, until a burning sensation mounted from my legs and attacked my lips and eyelids.

A drop of blood melted and slanted down her cheek. Her tongue quivered and receded. The laboured panting went on.

I could feel no pulse in her wrist, and put my ear against her frozen breast. Faintly, behind the raging blizzard, her heart was beating so fast that I could not count the beats, and I remained crouched over her, with my eyes closed. Something brushed my head – Rheya's hand in my hair. I stood up.

'Kris!' A harsh gasp.

I took her hand, and the answering pressure made my bones creak. Then her face screwed up with agony, and she lost consciousness again. Her eyes turned up, a guttural rattle tore at her throat, and her body arched with convulsions. It was all I could do to keep her on the operating-table; she broke free and her head cracked against a porcelain basin. I dragged her back, and struggled to hold her down, but violent spasms kept jerking her out of my grasp. I was pouring with sweat, and my legs were like jelly. When the convulsions abated, I tried to make her lie flat, but her chest thrust out to gulp at the air. Suddenly her eyes were staring out at me from behind the frightful blood-stained mask of her face.

'Kris . . . how long . . . how long?'

She choked. Pink foam appeared at her mouth, and the convulsions racked her again. With my last reserves of strength I bore down on her shoulders, and she fell back. Her teeth chattered loudly.

'No, no, no,' she whimpered suddenly, and I thought that death was near.

But the spasms resumed, and again I had to hold her down. Now and then she swallowed dryly, and her ribs heaved. Then the eyelids half closed over the unseeing eyes, and she stiffened. This must be the end. I did not even try to wipe the foam from her mouth. A distant ringing throbbed in my head. I was waiting for her final breath before my strength failed and I collapsed to the ground.

She went on breathing, and the rasp was now only a light sigh. Her chest, which had stopped heaving, moved again to the rapid rhythm of her heartbeat. Colour was returning to her cheeks. Still I did not realize what was happening. My hands were clammy, and I heard as if through layers of cotton-wool, yet the ringing sound continued.

Rheya's eyelids moved, and our eyes met.

I could not speak her name from behind the mask of my face. All I could do was look at her.

She turned her head and looked round the room. Somewhere behind me, in another world, a tap dripped. Rheya levered herself up on her elbow. I recoiled, and again our eyes met.

'It . . . it didn't work,' she stammered. 'Why are you looking at me like that?' Then she screamed out loud: 'Why are you looking at me like that?'

Still I could say nothing. She examined her hands, moved her fingers . . .

'Is this me?'

My lips formed her name, and she repeated it as a question – 'Rheya?'

She let herself slide off the operating-table, staggered,

regained her balance and took a few steps. She was moving in a daze, and looking at me without appearing to see me.

'Rheya? But . . . I am not Rheya. Who am I then? And you, what about you?' Her eyes widened and sparkled, and an astonished smile lit up her face. 'And you, Kris. Perhaps you too . . .'

I had backed away until I came up against the wall. The smile vanished.

'No. You are afraid. I can't take any more of this, I can't . . . I didn't know, I still don't understand. It's not possible.' Her clenched fists struck her chest. 'What else could I think, except that I was Rheya! Maybe you believe this is all an act? It isn't, I swear it isn't.'

Something snapped in my mind, and I went to put my arms round her, but she fought free:

'Don't touch me! Leave me alone! I disgust you, I know I do. Keep away! I'm not Rheya . . .'

We screamed at each other and Rheya tried to keep me at arm's length. I would not let her go, and at last she let her head fall to my shoulder. We were on our knees, breathless and exhausted.

'Kris . . . what do I have to do to put a stop to this?'

'Be quiet!'

'You don't know!' She lifted her head and stared at me. 'It can't be done, can it?'

'Please . . .'

'I really tried . . . No, go away. I disgust you – and myself, I disgust myself. If I only knew how . . .'

'You would kill yourself.'

'Yes.'

'But I want you to stay alive. I want you here, more than anything.'

'You're lying.'

'Tell me what I have to do to convince you. You are here. You exist. I can't see any further than that.'

148

'It can't possibly be true, because I am not Rheya.'

'Then who are you?'

There was a long silence. Then she bowed her head and murmured:

'Rheya . . . But I know that I am not the woman you once loved.'

'Yes. But that was a long time ago. That past does not exist, but you do, here and now. Don't you see?'

She shook her head:

'I know that it was kindness that made you behave as you did, but there is nothing to be done. That first morning when I found myself waiting by your bed for you to wake up, I knew nothing. I can hardly believe it was only three days ago. I behaved like a lunatic. Everything was misty. I didn't remember anything, wasn't surprised by anything. It was like recovering from a drugged sleep, or a long illness. It even occurred to me that I might have been ill and you didn't want to tell me. Then a few things happened to set me thinking – you know what I mean. So after you met that man in the library and you refused to tell me anything, I made up my mind to listen to that tape. That was the only time I have lied to you, Kris. When you were looking for the tape-recorder, I knew where it was. I'd hidden it. The man who recorded the tape – what was his name?'

'Gibarian.'

'Yes, Gibarian – he explained everything. Although I still don't understand. The only thing missing was that I can't . . . that there is no end. He didn't mention that, or if he did it was after you woke up and I had to switch off. But I heard enough to realize that I am not a human being, only an instrument.'

'What are you talking about?'

'That's what I am. To study your reactions – something of that sort. Each one of you has a . . . an instrument like me. We emerge from your memory or your imagination, I can't say

149

exactly – anyway you know better than I. He talks about such terrible things . . . so far fetched . . . if it did not fit in with everything else I would certainly have refused to believe him.'

'The rest?'

'Oh, things like not needing sleep, and being compelled to go wherever you go. When I think that only yesterday I was miserable because I thought you detested me. How stupid! But how could I have imagined the truth? He – Gibarian – didn't hate that woman, the one who came to him, but he refers to her in such a dreadful way. It wasn't until then that I realized that I was helpless whatever I did, and that I couldn't avoid torturing you. More than that though, an instrument of torture is passive, like the stone that falls on somebody and kills them. But an instrument of torture which loves you and wishes you nothing but good – it was too much for me. I wanted to tell you the little that I *had* understood. I told myself that it might be useful to you. I even tried to make notes . . .'

'That time when you had the light switched on?'

'Yes. But I couldn't write anything. I searched myself for . . . you know, some sign of "influence" . . . I was going mad. I felt as if there was no body underneath my skin and there was something else instead: as if I was just an illusion meant to mislead you. You see?'

'I see.'

'When you can't sleep at night and your mind keeps spinning for hours on end, it can take you far away; you find yourself moving in strange directions . . .'

'I know what you mean.'

'But I could feel my heart beating. And then I remembered that you had made an analysis of my blood. What did you find? You can tell me the truth now.'

'Your blood is like my own.'

'Truly?'

'I give you my word.'

'What does that indicate? I had been telling myself that the ... unknown force might be concealed somewhere inside me, and that it might not occupy very much space. But I did not know whereabouts it was. I think now that I was evading the real issue because I didn't have the nerve to make a decision. I was afraid, and I looked for a way out. But Kris, if my blood is like yours ... if I really ... no, it's impossible. I would already be dead, wouldn't I? That means there really is something different – but where? In the mind? Yet it seems to me that I think as any human being does . . and I know nothing! If that alien thing was thinking in my head, I would know everything. And I would not love you. I would be pretending, and aware that I was pretending. Kris, you've got to tell me everything you know. Perhaps we could work out a solution between us.'

'What kind of solution?' She fell silent. 'Is it death you want?'

'Yes, I think it is.'

Again silence. Rheya sat on the floor, her knees drawn up under her chin. I looked around at the white enamelled fittings and gleaming instruments, perhaps looking for some unsuspected clue to suddenly materialize.

'Rheya, I have something to say, too.' She waited quietly. 'It is true that we are not exactly alike. But there is nothing wrong with that. In any case, whatever else we might think about it, that ... difference ... saved your life.'

A painful smile flickered over her face: 'Does that mean that I am ... immortal?'

'I don't know. At any rate, you're far less vulnerable than I am.'

'It's horrible . . .'

'Perhaps not as horrible as you think.'

'But you don't envy me.'

'Rheya, I don't know what your fate will be. It cannot be predicted, any more than my own or any other members' of the Station's personnel. The experiment will go on, and anything can happen . . .'

'Or nothing.'

'Or nothing. And I have to confess that nothing is what I would prefer. Not because I'm frightened – though fear is undeniably an element of this business – but because there can't be any final outcome. I'm quite sure of that.'

'Outcome? You mean the ocean?'

'Yes, contact with the ocean. As I see it, the problem is basically very simple. Contact means the exchange of specific knowledge, ideas, or at least of findings, definite facts. But what if no exchange is possible? If an elephant is not a giant microbe, the ocean is not a giant brain. Obviously there can be various approaches, and the consequence of one of them is that you are here, now, with me. And I am trying my hardest to make you realize that I love you. Just your being here cancels out the twelve years of my life that went into the study of Solaris, and I want to keep you.

'You may have been sent to torment me, or to make my life happier, or as an instrument ignorant of its function, used like a microscope with me on the slide. Possibly you are here as a token of friendship, or a subtle punishment, or even as a joke. It could be all of those at once, or – which is more probable – something else completely. If you say that our future depends on the ocean's intentions, I can't deny it. I can't tell the future any more than you can. I can't even swear that I shall always love you. After what has happened already, we can expect anything. Suppose tomorrow it turns me into a green jellyfish! It's out of our hands. But the decision we make today is in our hands. Let's decide to stay together. What do you say?'

'Listen, Kris, there's something else I must ask you . . . Am I . . . do I look very like her?'

'You did at first. Now I don't know.'

'I don't understand.'

'Now all I see is you.'

'You're sure?'

'Yes. If you really were her, I might not be able to love you.'

'Why?'

'Because of what I did.'

'Did you treat her badly?'

'Yes, when we . . .'

'Don't say any more.'

'Why not?'

'So that you won't forget that I am the one who is here, not her.'

Conversation

The following morning, I received another note from Snow: Sartorius had left off working on the disruptor and was getting ready for a final experiment with high-power X-rays.

'Rheya, darling, I have to pay a visit to Snow.'

The red dawn blazing through the window divided the room in two. We were in an area of blue shadow. Everything outside this shadow-zone was burnished copper: if a book had fallen from a shelf; my ear would have listened instinctively for a metallic clang.

'It's to do with the experiment. Only I don't know what to do about it. Please understand, I'd rather . . .'

'You needn't justify yourself, Kris. If only it doesn't go on too long.'

'It's bound to take a while. Look, do you think you could wait in the corridor?'

'I can try. But what if I lose control?'

'What does it feel like? I'm not asking just out of curiosity, believe me, but if we can discuss how it works you might find some way of keeping it in check.'

Rheya had turned pale, but she tried to explain:

'I feel afraid, not of some thing or some person – there's no focus, only a sense of being lost. And I am terribly ashamed of myself. Then, when you come back, it stops. That's what made me think I might have been ill.'

'Perhaps it's only inside this damned Station that it works. I'll make arrangements for us to get out as soon as possible.'

'Do you think you can?'

'Why not? I'm not a prisoner here. I'll have to talk it over with Snow. Have you any idea how long you could manage to remain by yourself?'

'That depends . . . If I could hear your voice, I think I might be able to hold out.'

'I'd rather you weren't listening. Not that I have anything to hide, but there's no telling what Snow might say.'

'You needn't go on. I understand. I'll just stand close enough to hear the sound of your voice.'

'I'm going to the operating-room to phone him. The doors will be open.'

Rheya nodded agreement.

I crossed the red zone. The corridor seemed dark by contrast, in spite of the lighting. Inside the open door of the operating-room, fragments of the Dewar bottle, the last traces of the previous night's events, gleamed from under a row of liquid-oxygen containers. When I took the phone off the hook, the little screen lit up, and I tapped out the number of the radio-cabin. Behind the dull glass, a spot of bluish light grew, burst, and Snow was looking at me, perched on the edge of his chair.

'I got your note and I want to talk to you. Can I come over?'

'Yes. Right away?'

'Yes.'

'Excuse me, but are you coming alone or . . . accompanied?'

'Alone.'

His creased forehead and thin, tanned face filled the screen as he leant forward to scrutinize me through the convex glass. Then he appeared to reach an abrupt decision:

'Fine, fine, I'll be expecting you.'

I went back to the cabin, where I could barely make out the shape of Rheya behind the curtain of red sunlight. She was sitting in an armchair, with her hands clutching the arm-rests. She must have failed to hear my footsteps, and I saw her for a moment fighting the inexplicable compulsion that possessed her and wrestling with the fierce contractions of her entire body which stopped immediately she saw me. I choked back a feeling of blind rage and pity.

We walked in silence down the long corridor with its polychromed walls; the designers had intended the variations in colour to make life more tolerable inside the armoured shell of the Station. A shaft of red light ahead of us meant that the door of the radio-cabin was ajar, and I looked at Rheya. She made no attempt to return my smile, totally absorbed in her preparations for the coming battle with herself. Now that the ordeal was about to begin, her face was pinched and white. Fifteen paces from the door, she stopped, pushing me forward gently with her fingertips as I started to turn around. Suddenly I felt that Snow, the experiment, even the Station itself were not worth the agonizing price that Rheya was ready to pay, with myself as assistant torturer. I would have retraced my steps, but a shadow fell across the cabin doorway, and I hurried inside.

Snow stood facing me with the red sun behind him making a halo of purple light out of his grey hair. We confronted one another without speaking, and he was able to examine me at his leisure in the sunlight that dazzled me so that I could hardly see him.

I walked past him and leant against a tall desk bristling with microphones on their flexible stalks. Snow pivoted slowly and went on staring at me with his habitual cheerless smile, in which there was no amusement, only overpowering fatigue. Still with his eyes on mine, he picked his way through the piles of objects littered about the cabin – thermic cells, instruments, spare parts for the electronic equipment – pulled a stool up against the door of a steel cabinet, and sat down.

I listened anxiously, but no sound came from the corridor. Why did Snow not speak? The prolonged silence was becoming exasperating.

I cleared my throat:

'When will you and Sartorius be ready?'

'We can start today, but the recording will take some time.'

'Recording? You mean the encephalogram?'

'Yes, you agreed. Is anything wrong?'

'No, nothing.'

Another lengthening silence. Snow broke it:

'Did you have something to tell me?'

'She knows,' I whispered.

He frowned, but I had the impression that he was not really surprised. Then why pretend? I lost all desire to confide in him. All the same, I had to be honest:

'She started to suspect after our meeting in the library. My behaviour, various other indications. Then she found Gibarian's tape-recorder and played back the tape.'

Snow sat intent and unmoving. Standing by the desk, my view of the corridor was blocked by the half-open door. I lowered my voice again:

'Last night, while I was asleep, she tried to kill herself. She drank liquid oxygen . . .' There was a sound of rustling, like papers stirred by the wind. I stopped and listened for something in the corridor, but the noise did not come from there. A mouse in the cabin? Out of the question, this was Solaris. I stole a glance at Snow.

'Go on,' he said calmly.

'It didn't work, of course. Anyway, she knows who she is.'

'Why tell me?'

I was taken aback for an instant, then I stammered out:

'So as to inform you, to keep you up to date on the situation . . .'

'I warned you.'

'You mean you knew?' My voice rose involuntarily.

'What you have just told me? Of course not. But I explained the position. When it arrives, the visitor is almost blank – only a ghost made up of memories and vague images dredged out of its . . . source. The longer it stays with you, the more human it becomes. It also becomes more independent, up to a certain point. And the longer that goes on, thé more difficult it gets . . .'

157

Snow broke off, looked me up and down, and went on reluctantly: 'Does she know everything?'

'Yes, I've just told you.'

'Everything? Does she know that she came once before, and that you . . .'

'No!'

'Listen, Kelvin,' he smiled ruefully, 'if that's how it is, what do you want to do – leave the Station?'

'Yes.'

'With her?'

'Yes.'

The silence while he considered his reply also revealed something else. Again, from somewhere close, and without being able to pin it down, I heard the same faint rustling in the cabin, as if through a thin partition.

Snow shifted on his stool.

'All right. Why look at me like that? Do you think I would stand in your way? You can do as you like, Kelvin. We're in enough trouble already without putting pressure on each other. I know it will be a hopeless job to convince you, but there's something I have to say: you are doing all you can to stay human in an inhuman situation. Noble it may be, but it isn't going to get you anywhere. And I'm not so sure about it being noble – not if it's idiotic at the same time. But that's your affair. Let's get back to the point. You renege on the experiment and take her away with you. Has it struck you that you'll only be embarking on a different kind of experiment?'

'What do you mean? If you want to know whether she can manage it, as long as I'm with her, I don't see . . .' I trailed to a halt.

Snow sighed:

'All of us have our heads in the sand, Kelvin, and we know it. There's no need to put on airs.'

'I'm not putting anything on.'

'I'm sorry, I didn't want to offend you. I take back the

airs, but I still think that you are playing the ostrich game – and a particularly dangerous version. You deceive yourself, you deceive her, and you chase your own tail. Do you know the necessary conditions for stabilizing a neutrino field?'

'No, and nor do you. Nor does anyone.'

'Exactly. All we know is that the structure is inherently unstable, and can only be maintained by means of a continuous energy input. Sartorius told me that. This energy creates a rotating stabilization field. Now, does that energy come from outside the "visitor", or is it generated internally? You see the difference?'

'Yes. If it is external, she . . .'

Snow finished the sentence for me:

'Away from Solaris, the structure disintegrates. It's only a theory, of course, but one that you can verify, since you have already set up an experiment. The vehicle you launched is still in orbit. In my spare moments, I've even calculated its trajectory. You can take off, intercept, and find out what happened to the passenger . . .'

'You're out of your mind,' I yelled.

'You think so? And what if we brought the shuttle down again? No problem – it's on remote control. We'll bring it out of orbit, and . . .'

'Shut up!'

'That won't do either? There's another method, a very simple one. It doesn't involve bringing the shuttle down, only establishing radio contact. If she's alive, she'll reply, and . . .'

'The oxygen would have run out days ago.'

'She may not need it. Shall we try?'

'Snow . . . Snow . . .'

He mimicked my intonation angrily:

'Kelvin . . . Kelvin . . . Think, just a little. Are you a man or not? Who are you trying to please? Who do you want to save? Yourself? Her? And which version of her? This one or that one? Haven't you got the guts to face them both? Surely you realize that you haven't thought it through. Let me tell you one last time, we are in a situation that is beyond morality.'

The rustling noise returned, and this time it sounded like nails scraping on a wall. All at once I was filled with a dull indifference. I saw myself, I saw both of us, from a long way off, as if through the wrong end of a telescope, and everything looked meaningless, trivial and slightly ridiculous.

'So what do you suggest? Send up another shuttle? She would be back tomorrow. And the day after, and the day after that. How long do you want it to go on? What's the good of disposing of her if she keeps returning? How would it help me, or you, or Sartorius, or the Station?'

'No, here's my suggestion: leave with her. You'll witness the transformation. After a few minutes, you'll see . . .'

'What? A monster, a demon?'

'No, you'll see her die, that's all. Don't think that they are immortal – I promise you that they die. And then what will you do? Come back . . . for a fresh sample?' He stared at me with bantering condescension.

'That's enough!' I burst out, clenching my fists.

'Oh, I'm the one who has to be quiet? Look, I didn't start this conversation, and as far as I'm concerned it has gone on long enough. Let me just suggest some ways for you to amuse yourself. You could scourge the ocean with rods, for instance. You've got it into your head that you're a traitor if you . . .' He waved his hand in farewell, and raised his head as if to watch an imaginary ship in flight. '. . . and a good man if you keep her. Smiling when you feel like screaming, and shamming cheerful when you want to beat your head against a wall, isn't that being a traitor? What if it is not possible, here, to be anything but a traitor? What will you do? Take it out on that bastard Snow, who is the cause of it all? In that case, Kelvin, you just put the lid on the rest of your troubles by acting like a complete idiot!'

'You are talking from your own point of view. I love this girl.'

'Her memory, you mean?'

'No, herself. I told you what she tried to do. How many "real" human beings would have that much courage?'

'So you admit . . .'

'Don't quibble.'

'Right. So she loves you. And you want to love her. It isn't the same thing.'

'You're wrong.'

'I'm sorry, Kelvin, but it was your idea to spill all this. You don't love her. You do love her. She is willing to give her life. So are you. It's touching, it's magnificent, anything you like, but it's out of place here – it's the wrong setting. Don't you see? No, you don't want to. You are going around in circles to satisfy the curiosity of a power we don't understand and can't control, and she is an aspect, a periodic manifestation of that power. If she was . . . if you were being pestered by some infatuated hag, you wouldn't think twice about packing her off, right?'

'I suppose so.'

'Well then, that probably explains why she is not a hag! You feel as if your hands are tied? That's just it, they are!'

'All you are doing is adding one more theory to the millions of theories in the library. Leave me alone, Snow, she is . . . No, I won't say any more.'

'It's up to you. But remember that she is a mirror that reflects a part of your mind. If she is beautiful, it's because your memories are. You provide the formula. You can only finish where you started, don't forget that.'

'What do you expect me to do? Send her away? I've already asked you why, and you don't answer.'

'I'll give you an answer. It was you who wanted this conversation, not me. I haven't meddled with your affairs, and I'm not telling you what to do or what not to do. Even if I had the right, I would not. You come here of your own free will, and you dump it all on me. You know why? To take the weight off your own back. Well I've experienced that weight – don't try to shut me up – and I leave you free to find your own solution. But you *want* opposition. If I got in your way, you could fight me, something tangible, a man just like you, with the same flesh and blood. Fight me, and you could feel that you too were a man. When I don't give you the excuse to fight, you quarrel with me, or rather with yourself. The one thing you've left out is telling me you'd die of grief if *she* suddenly disappeared . . .No, please, I've heard enough!'

I countered clumsily:

'I came to tell you, because I thought you ought to know, that I intend leaving the Station with her.'

'Still on the same tack.' Snow shrugged. 'I only offered my opinion because I realized that you were losing touch with reality. And the further you go, the harder you fall. Can you come and see Sartorius around nine tomorrow morning?'

'Sartorius? I thought he wasn't letting anybody in. You told me you couldn't even phone him.'

'He seems to have reached some kind of settlement. We never discuss our domestic troubles. With you, it's another matter. Will you come tomorrow morning?'

'All right,' I grunted.

I noticed that Snow had slipped his left hand inside the cabinet. How long had the door been ajar? Probably for some time, but in the heat of the encounter I had not registered that the position of his hand was not natural. It was as if he was concealing something – or holding somebody's hand.

I licked my lips:

'Snow, what have you . . .'

'You'd better leave now,' he said evenly.

I closed the door in the final glow of the red twilight. Rheya was huddled against the wall a few paces down the corridor. She sprang to her feet at once:

'You see? I did it, Kris. I feel so much better . . . Perhaps it will be easier and easier . . .'

'Yes, of course . . .' I answered absently.

We went back to my quarters. I was still speculating about that cabinet, and what had been hiding there, perhaps overhearing our entire conversation. My cheeks started to burn so hard that I involuntarily passed the back of my hand over them. What an idiotic meeting! And where did it get us? Nowhere. But there was tomorrow morning . . .

An abrupt thrill of fear ran through me. My encephalogram, a complete record of the workings of my brain, was to be beamed into the ocean in the form of radiation. What was it Snow had said – would I suffer terribly if Rheya departed? An encephalogram records every mental process, conscious and unconscious. If I want her to disappear, will it happen? But if I wanted to get rid of her would I also be appalled at the thought of her imminent destruction? Am I responsible for my unconscious? No one else is, if not myself. How stupid to agree to let them do it. Obviously I can examine the recording before it is used, but I won't be able to decode it. Nobody could. The experts can only identify general mental tendencies. For instance, they will say that the subject is thinking about some mathematical problem, but they are unable to specify its precise terms. They claim that they have to stick to generalizations because the encephalogram cannot discriminate among the stream of simultaneous impulses, only some of which have any psychological 'counterpart', and they refuse point-blank to hazard any comment on the unconscious processes. So how could they be expected to decipher memories which have been more or less repressed?

Then why was I so afraid? I had told Rheya only that morning that the experiment could not work. If Terran neurophysiologists were incapable of decoding the recording, what chance was there for that great alien creature . . .?

Yet it had infiltrated my mind without my knowledge, surveyed my memory, and laid bare my most vulnerable point. That was undeniable. Without any assistance or

163

radiation transmissions, it had found its way through the armoured shell of the Station, located me, and come away with its spoils . . .

'Kris?' Rheya whispered.

Standing at the window with unseeing eyes, I had not noticed the coming of darkness. A thin ceiling of high cloud glowed a dim silver in the light of the vanished sun, and obscured the stars.

If she disappears after the experiment, that will mean that I wanted her to disappear – that I killed her. No, I will not see Sartorius. They can't force me to cooperate. But I can't tell them the truth, I'll have to dissemble and lie, and keep on doing it . . . Because there may be thoughts, intentions and cruel hopes in my mind of which I know nothing, because I am a murderer unawares. Man has gone out to explore other worlds and other civilizations without having explored his own labyrinth of dark passages and secret chambers, and without finding what lies behind doorways that he himself has sealed. Was I to abandon Rheya there out of false shame, or because I lacked the courage?

'Kris,' said Rheya, more softly still.

She was standing quite close to me now. I pretended not to hear. At that moment, I wanted to isolate myself. I had not yet resolved anything, or reached any decision. I stood motionless, looking at the dark sky and the cold stars, pale ghosts of the stars that shone on Earth. My mind was a blank. All I had was the grim certainty of having crossed some point of no return. I refused to admit that I was travelling towards what I could not reach. Apathy robbed me of the strength even to despise myself.

The Thinkers

'Kris, is it the experiment that's on your mind?'

The sound of her voice made me start with surprise. I had been lying in the dark for hours with my eyes open, unable to sleep. Not hearing Rheya's breathing, I had forgotten her, letting myself drift in a tide of aimless speculation. The waking dream had lured me out of sight of the measure and meaning of reality.

'How did you know I wasn't asleep?'

'Your breathing changes when you are asleep,' she said gently, as if to apologize for her question. 'I didn't want to interfere . . . If you can't answer, don't.'

'Why would I not tell you? Anyway you've guessed right, it is the experiment.'

'What do they expect to achieve?'

'They don't know themselves. Something. Anything. It isn't "Operation Brainwave", it's "Operation Desperation". Really, one of us ought to have the courage to call the experiment off and shoulder the responsibility for the decision, but the majority reckons that that kind of courage would be a sign of cowardice, and the first step in a retreat. They think it would mean an undignified surrender for mankind – as if there was any dignity in floundering and drowning in what we don't understand and never will.' I stopped, but a new access of rage quickly built up. 'Needless to say they're not short of arguments. They claim that even if we fail to establish contact we won't have been wasting our time investigating the plasma, and that we shall eventually uncover the secret of matter. They know very well that they are deceiving themselves. It's like wandering about in a library where all the books are written in an indecipherable language. The only thing that's familiar is the colour of the bindings!'

'Are there no other planets like this?'

'It's possible. This is the only one we've come across. In any case, it's in an extremely rare category, not like Earth. Earth is a common type – the grass of the universe! And we pride ourselves on this universality. There's nowhere we can't go; in that belief we set out for other worlds, all brimming with confidence. And what were we going to do with them? Rule them or be ruled by them: that was the only idea in our pathetic minds! What a useless waste . . .'

I got out of bed and fumbled in the medicine-cabinet. My fingers recognized the shape of the big bottle of sleeping pills, and I turned around in the darkness:

'I'm going to sleep, darling.' Up in the ceiling, the ventilator hummed. 'I must get some sleep . . .'

In the morning, I woke up feeling calm and refreshed. The experiment seemed a petty matter, and I could not understand how I had managed to take the encephalogram so seriously. Nor was I much bothered by having to bring Rheya into the laboratory. In spite of all her exertions, she could not bear to stay out of sight and earshot for longer than five minutes, so I had abandoned my idea of further tests (she was even prepared to let herself be locked up somewhere), asked her to come with me, and advised her to bring something to read.

I was especially curious about what I would find in the laboratory. There was nothing unusual about the appearance of the big, blue and white-painted room, except that the shelves and cupboards meant to contain glass instruments seemed bare. The glass panel in one door was starred, and in some doors it was missing altogether, suggesting that there had been a struggle here recently, and that someone had done his best to remove the traces.

Snow busied himself with the equipment, and behaved

quite civilly, showing no surprise at the sight of Rheya, and greeting her with a quick nod of the head.

I was lying down, and Snow was swabbing my temples and forehead with saline solution, when a narrow door opened and Sartorius emerged from an unlighted room. He was wearing a white smock and a black anti-radiation overall that came down to his ankles, and his greeting was authoritative and very professional in manner. We might have been two researchers in some great institute on Earth, continuing from where we had left off the day before. He was not wearing his dark glasses, but I noticed that he had on contact lenses, which I took to be the explanation of his lack of expression.

Sartorius looked on with arms folded as Snow attached the electrodes and wrapped a bandage around my head. He looked around the room several times, ignoring Rheya, who sat on a stool with her back against the wall, pretending to read.

Snow stepped back, and I moved my head, which was bulging with metal discs and wires, to watch him switch on. At this point Sartorius raised his hand and launched into a flowery speech:

'Dr. Kelvin, may I have your attention and concentration for a moment. I do not intend to dictate any precise sequence of thought to you, for that would invalidate the experiment, but I do insist that you cease thinking of yourself, of me, our colleague Snow, or anybody else. Make an effort to eliminate any intrusion of individual personalities, and concentrate on the matter in hand. Earth and Solaris; the body of scientists considered as a single entity, although generations succeed each other and man as an individual has a limited span; our aspirations, and our perseverance in the attempt to establish an intellectual contact; the long historic march of humanity, our own certitude of furthering that advance, and our determination to renounce all personal feelings in order to accomplish our mission; the sacrifices that we are prepared to make, and the hardships we stand ready to overcome . . . These are the themes that might properly occupy your awareness. The association of ideas does not depend entirely on your own will. However, the very fact of your presence here bears out the authenticity of the progression I have drawn to your attention. If you are unsure that you have acquitted yourself of your task, say so, I beg you, and our colleague Snow will make another recording. We have plenty of time.'

A dry little smile flickered over his face as he spoke these last words, but his expression remained morose. I was still trying to unravel the pompous phraseology which he had spun out with the utmost gravity.

Snow broke the lengthening silence:

'Ready, Kris?'

He was leaning with one elbow on the control-panel of the electro-encephalograph, looking completely relaxed. His confident tone reassured me, and I was grateful to him for calling me by my first name.

'Let's get started.' I closed my eyes.

A sudden panic had overwhelmed me after Snow had fixed the electrodes and walked over to the controls: now it disappeared just as suddenly. Through half-closed lids, I could see the red lights winking on the black control-panel. I was no longer aware of the damp, unpleasant touch of the crown of clammy electrodes. My mind was an empty grey arena ringed by a crowd of invisible onlookers massed on tiers of seats, attentive, silent, and emanating in their silence an ironic contempt for Sartorius and the Mission. What should I improvise for these spectators? . . . Rheya . . . I introduced her name cautiously, ready to withdraw it at once, but no protest came, and I kept going. I was drunk with grief and tenderness, ready to suffer prolonged sacrifices patiently. My mind was pervaded with Rheya, without a body or a face, but alive inside me, real and imperceptible. Suddenly, as if printed over that despairing presence, I saw in the grey shadow the learned, professorial face of Giese, the father of Solarist studies and of Solarists. I was not visualizing the nauseating mud-eruption which had swallowed up the gold-rimmed spectacles and carefully brushed moustache. I was seeing the engraving on the title-page of his classic work, and the close-hatched strokes against which the artist had made his head stand out – so like my father's, that head, not in its features but in its expression of old-fashioned wisdom and honesty, that I was finally no longer able to tell which of them was looking at me, my father or Giese. They were dead, and neither of them buried, but then deaths without burial are not uncommon in our time.

The image of Giese vanished, and I momentarily forgot the Station, the experiment, Rheya and the ocean. Recent memories were obliterated by the overwhelming conviction that these two men, my father and Giese, nothing but ashes now, had once faced up to the totality of their existence, and this conviction afforded a profound calm which annihilated the formless assembly clustered around the grey arena in the expectation of my defeat.

I heard the click of circuit-breakers, and light penetrated my eyelids, which blinked open. Sartorius had not budged from his previous position, and was looking at me. Snow had his back turned to operate the control-panel. I had the impression that he was amusing himself by making his sandals slap on the floor.

'Do you think that stage one has been successful, Dr Kelvin?' Sartorius enquired, in the nasal voice which I had come to detest.

'Yes.'

'Are you sure?' he persisted, obviously rather surprised, and perhaps even suspicious.

'Yes.'

My assurance and the bluntness of my answers made him lose his composure briefly.

'Oh . . . good,' he stammered.

Snow came over to me and started to unwrap the bandage from my head. Sartorius stepped back, hesitated, then disappeared into the darkroom.

I was rubbing the circulation back into my legs when he came out again, holding the developed film. Zigzag lines traced a lacy pattern along fifty feet of glistening black ribbon. My presence was no longer necessary, but I stayed, and Snow fed the ribbon into the modulator. Sartorius made a final suspicious examination of the last few feet of the spool, as if trying to decipher the content of the wavering lines.

The experiment proceeded with a minimum of fuss. Snow and Sartorius each sat at a bank of controls and pushed buttons. Through the reinforced floor, I heard the whine of power building up in the turbines. Lights moved downward inside glass-fronted indicators in time with the descent of the great X-ray beamer to the bottom of its housing. They came to a stop at the low limit of the indicators.

Snow stepped up the power, and the white needle of the voltmeter described a left-to-right semicircle. The hum of current was barely audible now, as the film unwound, invisible behind the two round caps. Numbers clicked through the footage indicator.

I went over to Rheya, who was watching us over her book. She glanced up at me enquiringly. The experiment was over, and Sartorius was walking towards the heavy conical head of the machine.

'Can we go?' Rheya mouthed silently.

I replied with a nod, Rheya stood up, and we left the room without taking leave of my colleagues.

A superb sunset was blazing through the windows of the upper-deck corridor. Usually the horizon was reddish and gloomy at this hour. This time it was a shimmering pink, laced with silver. Under the soft glow of the light, the sombre foothills of the ocean shone pale violet. The sky was red only at the zenith.

We came to the bottom of the stairway, and I stopped,

reluctant to wall myself up again in the prison cell of the cabin.

'Rheya, I want to look something up in the library. Do you mind?'

'Of course not,' she exclaimed, in a forced attempt at cheerfulness. 'I can find myself something to read . . .'

I knew only too well that a gulf had opened between us since the previous day. I should have behaved more considerately, and tried to master my apathy, but I could not summon the strength.

We walked down the ramp leading to the library. There were three doors giving on to the little entrance hall, and crystal globes containing flowers were spaced out along the walls. I opened the middle door, which was lined with synthetic leather on either side. I always avoided contact with this upholstery when entering the library. We were greeted by a pleasant gust of fresh air. In spite of the stylized sun painted on the ceiling, the great circular hall had remained cool.

Idly running a finger along the spines of the books, I was on the point of choosing, out of all the Solarist classics, the first volume of Giese, so as to refresh my memory of the portrait on the title-page, when I came upon a book I had not noticed before, an octavo volume with a cracked binding. It was Gravinsky's *Compendium*, used mostly by students, as a crib.

Sitting in an armchair, with Rheya at my side, I leafed through Gravinsky's alphabetical classification of the various Solarist theories. The compiler, who had never set foot on Solaris, had combed through every monograph, expedition report, fragmentary outline and provisional account, even making excerpts of incidental comments about Solaris in planetological works dealing with other worlds. He had drawn up an inventory crammed with simplistic formulations, which grossly diminished the subtlety of the ideas it resumed. Originally intended as an all-embracing account,

Gravinsky's book was little more than a curiosity now. It had only been published twenty years before, but since that time such a mass of new theories had accumulated that there would not have been room for them in a single volume. I glanced through the index – practically an obituary list, for few of the authors cited were still alive, and among the survivors none was still playing an active part in Solarist studies. Reading all these names, and adding up the sum of the intellectual efforts they represented in every field of research, it was tempting to think that surely one of the theories quoted must be correct, and that the thousands of listed hypotheses must each contain some grain of truth, could not be totally unrelated to the reality.

In his introduction, Gravinsky divided the first sixty years of Solarist studies into periods. During the initial period, which began with the scouting ship that studied the planet from orbit, nobody had produced theories in the strict sense. 'Common sense' suggested that the ocean was a lifeless chemical conglomerate, a gelatinous mass which through its 'quasi-volcanic' activity produced marvellous creations and stabilized its eccentric orbit by virtue of a self-generated mechanical process, as a pendulum keeps itself on a fixed path once it is set in motion. To be precise, Magenon had come up with the idea that the 'colloidal machine' was alive three years after the first expedition, but according to the *Compendium* the period of biological hypotheses does not begin until nine years later, when Magenon's idea had acquired numerous supporters. The following years teemed with theoretical accounts of the living ocean, extremely complex, and supported by biomathematical analysis. During the third period, scientific opinion, hitherto practically unanimous, became divided.

What followed was internecine warfare between scores of new schools of thought. It was the age of Panmaller, Strobel, Freyus, Le Greuille and Osipowicz: the entire legacy of Giese was submitted to a merciless examination. The first atlases and inventories appeared, and new techniques in remote control enabled instruments to transmit stereophotographs from the interior of the asymmetriads, once considered impossible to explore. In the hubbub of controversy, the 'minimal' hypotheses were contemptuously dismissed: even if the long-awaited contact with the 'reasoning monster' did not materialize, it was argued that it was still worth investigating the cartilaginous cities of the mimoids and the ballooning mountains that rose above the ocean because we would gain valuable chemical and physio-chemical information, and enlarge our understanding of the structure of giant molecules. Nobody bothered even to refute the adherents of this defeatist line of reasoning. Scientists devoted themselves to drawing up catalogues of the typical metamorphoses which are still standard works, and Frank developed his bioplasmatic theory of the mimoids, which has since been shown to be inaccurate, but remains a superb example of intellectual audacity and logical construction.

The thirty or so years of the first three 'Gravinsky periods,' with their open assurance and irresistibly optimistic romanticism, constitute the infancy of Solarist studies. Already a growing scepticism heralded the age of maturity. Towards the end of the first quarter-century the early colloido-mechanistic theories had found a distant descendant in the concept of the 'apsychic ocean', a new and almost unanimous orthodoxy which threw overboard the view of that entire generation of scientists who believed that their observations were evidence of a conscious will, teleological processes, and activity motivated by some inner need of the ocean. This point of view was now overwhelmingly repudiated, and the ground was cleared for the team headed by Holden, Ionides and Stoliva, whose lucid, analytically based speculations concentrated on scrupulous examination of a growing body of data. It was the golden age of the archivists. Microfilm libraries burst at the seams with documents; expeditions, some of them more than a thousand strong, were equipped with the most lavish apparatus Earth could provide – robot recorders, sonar and radar, and the entire range of spectrometers, radiation counters and so on. Material was being accumulated at an accelerating tempo, but the essential spirit of the research flagged, and in the course of this period, still an optimistic one in spite of everything, a decline set in.

The first phase of Solaristics had been shaped by the personality of men like Giese, Strobel and Sevada, who had remained adventurous whether they were asserting or attacking a theoretical position. Sevada, the last of the great Solarists, disappeared near the south pole of the planet, and his death was never satisfactorily explained. He fell victim to a mistake which not even a novice would have made. Flying at low altitude, in full view of scores of observers, his aircraft had plunged into the interior of an agilus which was not even directly in its path. There was speculation about a sudden heart attack or fainting fit, or a mechanical failure, but I have always believed that this was in fact the first suicide, brought on by the first abrupt crisis of despair.

There were other 'crises', not mentioned in Gravinsky, whose details I was able to fill in out of my own knowledge as I stared at the yellowed, closely printed pages.

The later expressions of despair were in any case less dramatic, just as outstanding personalities became rarer. The recruitment of scientists to any particular field of study in a given age has never been studied as a phenomenon in its own right. Every generation throws up a fairly constant number of brilliant and determined men; the only difference lies in the direction they choose to take. The absence or presence of such individuals in a particular field of study is probably explicable in terms of the new perspectives offered. Opinions may differ about the researchers of the classical age of Solarist studies, but nobody can deny their stature, even their genius. For several decades, the mysterious ocean had attracted the best mathematicians and physicists, and the top specialists in biophysics, information theory and electro-physiology. Now, without warning, the army of researchers found itself leaderless. There remained a faceless mass of industrious collectors and compilers. The occasional original experiment might be devised, but the succession of vast expeditions mounted on a worldwide scale petered out, and the scientific world no longer echoed with ambitious, con-troversial theories.

The machinery of Solaristics fell into disrepair, and rusted over with hypotheses differentiated only in minor details, and unanimous in their concentration on the theme of the ocean's degeneration, regression and introversion. Now and then a bolder, more interesting concept might emerge, but it always amounted to a kind of indictment of the ocean, viewed as the end-product of a development which long ago, thousands of years before, had gone through a phase of superior organization, and now had nothing more than a physical unity. The argument went that its many useless, absurd creations were its death-throes – impressive enough, nonetheless – which had been going on for centuries. Thus, for instance, the extensors and mimoids were seen as tumours, and all the surface processes of the huge fluid body as expressions of chaos and anarchy. This approach to the problem became an obsession. For seven or eight years, the academic literature produced a spate of assertions which although framed in polite, cautious terms, amounted to little more than insults, the revenge of a rabble of leaderless suitors when they realized that the object of their most press-ing attentions was indifferent to the point of obstinately ignoring all their advances.

A group of European psychologists once carried out a pub-lic opinion poll spread over a period of several years. Their report had no direct bearing on Solarist studies, and was not included in the library collection, but I had read it, and retained a clear memory of its findings. The investigators had strikingly demonstrated that the changes in lay opinion were closely correlated to the fluctuations of opinion recorded in scientific circles.

That change was expressed even in the coordinating committee of the Institute of Planetology, which controls the financial appropriations for research, by means of a progressive reduction in the budgets of institutes and appointments devoted to Solarist studies, as well as by restrictions on the size of the exploration teams.

Some scientists adopted a position at the other extreme, and agitated for more vigorous steps to be taken. The administrative director of the Universal Cosmological Institute ventured to assert that the living ocean did not despise men in the least, but had not noticed them, as an elephant neither feels nor sees the ants crawling on its back. To attract and hold the ocean's attention, it would be necessary to devise more powerful stimuli, and gigantic machines tailored to the dimensions of the entire planet. Malicious commentators were not slow to point out that the director could well afford to be generous, since it was the Institute of Planetology which would have had to foot the bill.

Still the hypotheses rained down – old, 'resurrected' hypotheses, superficially modified, simplified, or complicated to the extreme – and Solaristics, a relatively well-defined discipline in spite of its scope, became an increasingly tangled maze where every apparent exit led to a dead end. In the climate of general indifference, stagnation and despondency, the ocean of Solaris was submerging under an ocean of printed paper.

Two years before I began the stint in Gibarian's laboratory which ended when I obtained the diploma of the Institute, the Mett-Irving Foundation offered a huge prize to anybody who could find a viable method of tapping the energy of the ocean. The idea was not a new one. Several cargoes of the plasmatic jelly had been shipped back to Earth in the past, and various methods of preservation had been patiently tested: high and low temperatures, artificial micro-atmospheres and micro-climates, and prolonged irradiation. The whole gamut of physical and chemical processes had been run, only to end with the same outcome, a gradual process of decomposition which passed through well-defined stages, starting with wasting, maceration, then first-degree (primary) and late (secondary) liquefaction. The samples removed from the plasmatic growths and creations met with the same fate, with certain variations in the phases of decomposition. The end-product was always a light metallic ash.

Once the scientists recognized that it was impossible to keep alive, or even in a 'vegetative' state, any fragment of the ocean, large or small, in dissociation from the entire organism, a growing tendency developed (under the influence of the Meunier-Proroch school) to isolate this problem as the key to the mystery. It was seen as a matter of interpretation – solve it, and the back of the problem would be broken.

The quest for this key, the philosopher's stone of Solarist studies, had absorbed the time and energy of all kinds of people with little or no scientific training. During the fourth decade of Solaristics the craze spread like an epidemic, and provided a fertile ground for the psychologists. An unknown number of cranks and ignorant fanatics toiled at their fumbling researches with a greater enthusiasm than any which had animated the old prophets of perpetual motion, or the squaring of the circle. The craze fizzled out in only a few years, and by the time I was ready to leave for Solaris it had vanished from the headlines and from conversation, and the ocean itself was practically forgotten by the public.

I took care to replace the *Compendium* in its correct alphabetical position, and in doing so dislodged a slim pamphlet by Grastrom, one of the most eccentric authors in Solarist literature. I had read the pamphlet, which was dictated by the urge to understand what lies beyond the grasp of mankind, and aimed in particular against the individual, man, and the human species. It was the abstract, acidulous work of an autodidact who had previously made a series of unusual contributions to various marginal and rarefied branches of quantum physics. In this fifteen-page booklet (his magnum opus!), Grastrom set out to demonstrate that the most abstract achievements of science, the most advanced theories and victories of mathematics represented nothing more than a stumbling, one- or two-step progression from our rude, prehistoric, anthropomorphic understanding of the universe around us. He pointed out correspondences with the human body – the projections of our senses, the structure of our physical organization, and the physiological limitations of man – in the equations of the theory of relativity, the theorem of magnetic fields and the various unified field theories. Grastrom's conclusion was that there neither was, nor could be, any question of 'contact' between mankind and any non-human civilization. This broadside against humanity made no specific mention of the living ocean, but its constant presence and scornful, victorious silence could be felt between every line, at any rate such had been my own impression. It was Gibarian who drew it to my attention, and it must have been Gibarian who had added it to the Station's collection, on his own authority, since Grastrom's pamphlet was regarded more as a curiosity than a true contribution to Solarist literature.

With a strange feeling almost of respect, I carefully slid the slim pamphlet back into the crowded bookshelf, then stroked the green bronze binding of the *Solaris Annual* with my fingertips. In the space of a few days, we had unquestionably gained positive information about a number of basic questions, which had made seas of ink flow and fed innumerable controversies, yet had remained sterile for lack of arguments. Today the mystery practically had us under siege, and we had powerful arguments.

Was the ocean a living creature? It could hardly be

doubted any longer by any but lovers of paradox or obstin-
acy. It was no longer possible to deny the 'psychic' functions of the ocean, no matter how that term might be defined.
Certainly it was only too obvious that the ocean had
'noticed' us. This fact alone invalidated that category of
Solarist theories which claimed that the ocean was an 'intro-
verted' world, a 'hermit entity', deprived by a process of
degeneration of the thinking organs it once possessed,
unaware of the existence of external objects and events, the
prisoner of a gigantic vortex of mental currents created and
confined in the depths of this monster revolving between
two suns.

Not only that, we had discovered that the ocean was capable of reproducing what we ourselves had never succeeded
in creating artificially – a perfect human body, modified in its
sub-atomic structure for purposes we could not guess.

The ocean lived, thought and acted. The 'Solaris problem'
had not been annihilated by its very absurdity. We were
truly dealing with a living creature. The 'lost' faculty was
not lost at all. All this now seemed proved beyond doubt.
Like it or not, men must pay attention to this neighbour, light
years away, but nevertheless a neighbour situated inside our
sphere of expansion, and more disquieting than all the rest of
the universe.

Perhaps we had arrived at a turning-point. What would
the high-level decision be? Would we be ordered to give up
and return to Earth, immediately or in the near future? Was it
even possible that we would be ordered to liquidate the
Station? It was at least not improbable. But I did not favour the
solution by retreat. The existence of the thinking colossus
was bound to go on haunting men's minds. Even when man
had explored every corner of the cosmos, and established
relations with other civilizations founded by creatures similar to ourselves, Solaris would remain an eternal challenge.

Misplaced among the thick volumes of the *Annual*, I discovered a small calf-bound book, and scanned its scuffed,

worn cover for a moment. It was Muntius's *Introduction to Solaristics*, published many years before. I had read it in a single night, after Gibarian had smilingly lent me his personal copy; and when I had turned the final page the light of a new Earth dawn was shining through my window. According to Muntius, Solaristics is the space era's equivalent of religion: faith disguised as science. Contact, the stated aim of Solaristics, is no less vague and obscure than the communion of the saints, or the second coming of the Messiah. Exploration is a liturgy using the language of methodology; the drudgery of the Solarists is carried out only in the expectation of fulfilment, of an Annunciation, for there are not and cannot be any bridges between Solaris and Earth. The comparison is reinforced by obvious parallels: Solarists reject arguments – no experiences in common, no communicable notions – just as the faithful rejected the arguments that undermined the foundations of their belief. Then again, what can mankind expect or hope for out of a joint 'pooling of information' with the living ocean? A catalogue of the vicissitudes associated with an existence of such infinite duration that it probably has no memory of its origins? A description of the aspirations, passions and sufferings that find expression in the perpetual creation of living mountains? The apotheosis of mathematics, the revelation of plenitude in isolation and renunciation? But all this represents a body of incommunicable knowledge. Transposed into any human language, the values and meanings involved lose all substance; they cannot be brought intact through the barrier. In any case, the 'adepts' do not expect such revelations – of the order of poetry, rather than science – since unconsciously it is Revelation itself that they expect, and this revelation is to explain to them the meaning of the destiny of man! Solaristics is a revival of long-vanished myths, the expression of mystical nostalgias which men are unwilling to confess openly. The cornerstone is deeply entrenched in the foundations of the edifice: it is the hope of Redemption.

Solarists are incapable of recognizing this truth, and consequently take care to avoid any interpretation of Contact, which is presented in their writings as an ultimate goal, whereas originally it had been considered as a beginning, and as a step on to a new path, among many other possible paths. Over the years, Contact has become sanctified. It has become the heaven of eternity.

Muntius analyses this 'heresy' of planetology very simply and trenchantly. He brilliantly dismantles the Solarist myth, or rather the myth of the Mission of Mankind.

Muntius's had been the first voice raised in protest, and had encountered the contemptuous silence of the experts, at a time when they still retained a romantic confidence in the development of Solaristics. After all, how could they have accepted a thesis that struck at the foundations of their achievements?

Solaristics went on waiting for the man who would reestablish it on a firm foundation and define its frontiers with precision. Five years after the death of Muntius, when his pamphlet had become a rare collectors' piece, a group of Norwegian researchers founded a school named after him. In contact with the personalities of his various spiritual heirs, the quiet thought of the master went through profound transformations; it led to the corrosive irony of Erle Ennesson and, on a more mundane plane, the 'utilitarian' or 'utilitarianistic' Solaristics of Fa-leng, who argued that science should settle for the immediate advantages offered by exploration, and not concern itself with any intellectual communion of two civilizations, or some illusory contact. Compared with the ruthless, lucid analysis of Muntius, the works of his disciples are hardly more than compilations and sometimes vulgarizations, with the exception of Ennesson's essays and perhaps the studies of Takata. Muntius himself had already defined the complete development of Solarist concepts. He called the first phase the era of the 'prophets', among whom he included Giese, Holden and Sevada; the second, the 'great schism' – the fragmentation of the one Solarist church into a number of warring sects; and he anticipated a third phase, which would set in when there was nothing left to investigate, and manifest itself in a crabbed, academic dogmatism. This prophecy was to prove inaccurate, however. In my opinion, Gibarian was right to characterize Muntius's strictures as a monumental simplification which ignored all the aspects of Solarist studies that had nothing in common with a creed, since the work of interpretation based itself only on the concrete evidence of a globe orbiting two suns.

Slipped between two pages of Muntius's pamphlet, I discovered an off-print of the quarterly review *Parerga Solariana*, which turned out to be one of the first articles written by Gibarian, even before he was appointed director of the Institute. The article was called 'Why I am a Solarist' and began with a concise account of all the material phenomena which confirmed the possibility of Contact. Gibarian belonged to that generation of researchers who had been daring and optimistic enough to hark back to the golden age, and who did not disown their own version of a faith that overstepped the frontiers imposed by science, and yet remained concrete, since it presupposed the success of perseverance.

Gibarian had been influenced by the classical work in bio-electronics for which the Eurasian school of Cho Enmin, Ngyalla and Kawakadze is famous. Their studies established an analogy between the charted electrical activity of the brain and certain discharges occurring deep in the plasma before the appearance, for example, of elementary polymorphs or twin solarids. Gibarian was opposed to anthropomorphizing interpretations, and the mystifications of the psychoanalytic, psychiatric and neurophysiological schools which attempted to endow the ocean with the symptoms of human illnesses, epilepsy among them (supposed to correspond with the spasmodic eruptions of the asymmetriads).

He was one of the most cautious and logical proponents of Contact, and saw no advantage in the kind of sensationalism which was in any case becoming more and more rare as applied to Solaris.

My own doctoral thesis received a fair amount of attention, not all of it welcome. It was based on the discoveries of Bergmann and Reynolds, who had succeeded in isolating and 'filtering' the elements of the most powerful emotions – despair, grief and pleasure – out of the mass of general mental processes. Systematically comparing their recordings with the electrical discharges from the ocean, I had observed oscillations in certain parts of symmetriads and at the bases of nascent mimoids which were sufficiently analogous to deserve further investigation. The journalists pounced on my thesis, and in some newspapers my name was coupled with grotesque headlines – 'The Despairing Jelly', 'The Planet in Orgasm'. But this dubious fame did have the fortunate consequence (or so I had thought a few days previously) of attracting the attention of Gibarian, who naturally could not read every new publication dealing with Solaris. The letter he sent me ended a chapter of my life, and began a new one . . .

The Dreams

When six days passed with no reaction from the ocean, we decided to repeat the experiment. Until now, the Station had been located at the intersection of the 43rd parallel and the 116th meridian. We moved south, maintaining a constant altitude of 1200 feet above the ocean – our radar confirmed automatic observations relayed by the artificial satellite which indicated a build-up of activity in the plasma of the southern hemisphere.

Forty-eight hours later, a beam of X-rays modulated by my own brain-patterns was bombarding the almost motionless surface of the ocean at regular intervals.

At the end of this two-day journey we had reached the outskirts of the polar region. The disc of the blue sun was setting to one side of the horizon, while on the opposite side billowing purple clouds announced the dawn of the red sun. In the sky, blinding flames and showers of green sparks clashed with the dull purple glow. Even the ocean participated in the battle between the two stars, here glittering with mercurial flashes, there with crimson reflections. The smallest cloud passing overhead brightened the shining foam on the wave-crests with iridescence. The blue sun had barely set when, at the meeting of ocean and sky, indistinct and drowned in blood-red mist (but signalled immediately by the detectors), a symmetriad blossomed like a gigantic crystal flower. The Station held its course, and after fifteen minutes the colossal ruby throbbing with dying gleams was once again hidden beneath the horizon. Some minutes later, a thin column spouted thousands of yards upwards into the atmosphere, its base obscured from view by the curvature of the planet. This fantastic tree, which went on growing and gushing blood and quicksilver, marked the end of the symmetriad: the tangled branches at the top of the column melted into a huge mushroom shape, illuminated by both suns simultaneously, and carried on the wind, while the lower part bulged, broke up into heavy clusters, and slowly sank. The death-throes lasted well over an hour.

Another two days passed. Our X-rays had irradiated a vast stretch of the ocean, and we made a final repetition of the experiment. From our observation post we spotted a chain of islets 250 miles to the south – six rocky promontories encrusted with a snowy substance which was in fact a deposit of organic origin, proving that the mountainous formation had once been part of the ocean bed.

We then moved south-west, and skirted a chain of mountains capped by clouds which gathered during the red day, and then disappeared. Ten days had elapsed since the first experiment.

On the surface, not much was happening in the Station. Sartorius had programmed the experiment for automatic repetition at set intervals. I did not even know whether anybody was checking the apparatus for correct function. In fact, the calm was not as complete as it seemed, but not because of any human activity.

I was afraid that Sartorius had no real intention of abandoning the construction of the disruptor. And how would Snow react when he found out that I had kept information from him and exaggerated the dangers we might run in the attempt to annihilate neutrino structures? Yet neither of the two said anything further about the project, and I kept wondering why they were so silent. I vaguely suspected them of keeping something from me – perhaps they had been working in secret – and every day I inspected the room which housed the disruptor, a windowless cell situated directly underneath the main laboratory. I never found anybody in the room, and the layer of dust over the armatures and cables of the apparatus proved that it had not been touched for weeks.

As a matter of fact, I did not meet anybody anywhere, and could not get through to Snow any more: nobody answered when I tried to call the radio-cabin. Somebody had to be controlling the Station's movements, but who? I had no idea, and oddly enough I considered the question was out of my province. The absence of response from the ocean left me equally indifferent, so much so that after two or three days I had stopped being either hopeful or apprehensive, and had completely written off the experiment and its possible results.

For days on end, I remained sitting in the library or in my cabin, accompanied by the silent shadow of Rheya. I was aware that there was an unease between us, and that my state of mindless suspension could not go on for ever. Obviously it was up to me to break the stalemate, but I resisted the very idea of any kind of change: I was incapable of making the most trivial decision. Everything inside the Station, and my relationship with Rheya in particular, felt fragile and insubstantial, as if the slightest alteration could shatter the perilous equilibrium and bring down ruin. I could not tell where this feeling originated, and the strangest thing of all is that Rheya too had a similar experience. When I look back on those moments today, I have a strong conviction that this atmosphere of uncertainty and suspense, and my presentiment of impending disaster, was provoked by an invisible presence which had taken possession of the Station. I believe too that I can claim that this presence manifested itself just as powerfully in dreams. I have never had visions of that kind before or since, so I decided to note them down and to transcribe them approximately, in so far as my vocabulary permits, given that I can convey only fragmentary glimpses almost entirely denuded of an incommunicable horror.

A blurred region, in the heart of vastness, far from earth and heaven, with no ground underfoot, no vault of sky overhead, nothing. I am the prisoner of an alien matter and my body is clothed in a dead, formless substance – or rather I have no body, I *am* that alien matter. Nebulous pale pink globules surround me, suspended in a medium more opaque than air, for objects only become clear at very close range, although when they do approach they are abnormally distinct, and their presence comes home to me with a preternatural vividness. The conviction of its substantial, tangible reality is now so overwhelming that later, when I wake up, I have the impression that I have just left a state of true perception, and everything I see after opening my eyes seems hazy and unreal.

That is how the dream begins. All around me, something is awaiting my consent, my inner acquiescence, and I know, or rather the knowledge exists, that I must not give way to an unknown temptation, for the more the silence seems to promise, the more terrible the outcome will be. Yet I essentially know no such thing, because I would be afraid if I knew, and I never felt the slightest fear.

I wait. Out of the enveloping pink mist, an invisible object emerges, and touches me. Inert, locked in the alien matter that encloses me, I can neither retreat nor turn away, and still I am being touched, my prison is being probed, and I feel this contact like a hand, and the hand re-creates me. Until now, I thought I saw, but had no eyes: now I have eyes! Under the caress of the hesitant fingers, my lips and cheeks emerge from the void, and as the caress goes further I have a face, breath stirs in my chest – I exist. And re-created, I in my turn create: a face appears before me that I have never seen until now, at once mysterious and known. I strain to meet its gaze, but I cannot impose any direction on my own, and we discover one another mutually, beyond any effort of will, in an absorbed silence. I have become alive again, and I feel as if there is no limitation on my powers. This creature – a woman? – stays near me, and we are motionless. The beat of our hearts combines, and all at once, out of the surrounding void where nothing exists or can exist, steals a presence of indefinable, unimaginable cruelty. The caress that created us and which wrapped us in a golden cloak becomes the crawling of innumerable fingers. Our white, naked bodies dissolve into a swarm of black creeping things, and I am – we are – a mass of glutinous coiling worms, endless, and in that infinity, no, I am infinite, and I howl soundlessly, begging for death and for an end. But simultaneously I am dispersed in all directions, and my grief expands in a suffering more acute than any waking state, a pervasive, scattered pain piercing the distant blacks and reds, hard as rock and ever-increasing, a mountain of grief visible in the dazzling light of another world.

That dream was one of the simplest. I cannot describe the others, for lack of a language to convey their dread. In those dreams, I was unaware of the existence of Rheya, nor was there any echo of past or recent events.

There were also visionless dreams, where in an unmoving, clotted silence I felt myself being slowly and minutely explored, although no instrument or hand touched me. Yet I felt myself being invaded through and through, I crumbled, disintegrated, and only emptiness remained. Total annihilation was succeeded by such terror that its memory alone makes my heart beat faster today.

So the days passed, each one like the next. I was indifferent to everything, fearing only the night and unable to find a means of escape from the dreams. Rheya never slept. I lay beside her, fighting against sleep, and the tenderness with which I clung to her was only a pretext, a way of avoiding the moment when I would be compelled to close my eyes. I had not mentioned these nightmares to her, but she must have guessed, for her attitude involuntarily betrayed a sense of deep humiliation.

As I say, I had not seen Snow or Sartorius for some time, yet Snow gave occasional signs of life. He would leave a note at my door, or call me on the videophone, asking whether I had noticed any new event or change, or anything at all which could be interpreted as a response to the repeated X-ray bombardments. I told him no, and asked him the same question, but there in the little screen Snow only shook his head.

On the fifteenth day after the conclusion of the experiment, I woke up earlier than usual, exhausted by the previous night's dreams. All my limbs were numbed, as if emerging from the effects of a powerful narcotic. The first rays of the red sun shone through the window, a blanket of red flame rippled over the surface of the ocean, and I realized that the vast expanse which had not been disturbed by the slightest movement in the past four days was beginning to stir. The dark ocean was abruptly covered by a thin veil of mist which seemed at the same time to have a very palpable consistency. Here and there the mist shook, and tremors spread out to the horizon in all directions. Now the ocean disappeared altogether beneath thick, corrugated membranes with pink swellings and pearly depressions, and these strange waves suspended above the ocean swirled suddenly and coalesced into great balls of blue-green foam. A tempest of wind hurled them upwards to the height of the Station, and wherever I looked, immense membranous wings were soaring in the red sky. Some of these wings of foam, which blotted out the sun, were pitch black, and others shone with highlights of purple as they were exposed obliquely to the sunlight. Still the phenomenon continued, as if the ocean were mutating, or shedding an old scaly skin. Now and again the dark surface of the ocean could be glimpsed through a gap that the foam filled in an instant. Wings of foam planed all around me, only a few yards from the window, and one swooped to rub against the window pane like a silken scarf. As the ocean went on giving birth to these fantastic birds, the first flights were already dissipating high above, decomposing at their zenith into transparent filaments.

The Station remained motionless as long as the spectacle lasted – about three hours, until night intervened. And even after the sun had set and the shadows had spread over the ocean, the lurid glow of myriad wings could still be discerned rising into the sky, hovering in massed ranks, and climbing effortlessly towards the light.

This performance had terrified Rheya, but it was no less disconcerting for me, although its novelty ought not to have been disturbing, since two or three times a year, and oftener when luck smiled on them, Solarists observed forms and creations never previously recorded.

The following night, an hour before the blue sunrise, we witnessed another effect: the ocean was becoming phosphorescent. Pools of grey light were rising and falling to the rhythm of invisible waves. Isolated at first, these grey patches quickly spread and joined together, and soon made up a carpet of spectral light extending as far as the eye could see. The intensity of the light grew progressively for some fifteen to twenty minutes, then the phenomenon came to a surprising end. A pall of shadow approached from the west, stretching along a front several hundred miles wide. When this moving shadow had overtaken the Station, the phosphorescent part of the ocean, retreating eastward, seemed to be trying to escape from the vast extinguisher. It was like an aurora put to flight, and retreating as far as the horizon, which was edged by a fading glow before the darkness conquered. Shortly afterwards, the sun rose above the ocean wastes, which were furrowed by a few solidified waves, whose mercurial reflections played on my window.

The phosphorescence was a recorded effect, sometimes observed before the eruption of an asymmetriad, but always indicative of a local increase in the activity of the plasma. Nevertheless, in the course of the next two weeks nothing happened either inside or outside the Station, except on one occasion when in the middle of the night I heard the sound of a piercing scream which came from no human throat. The shrill, protracted howling woke me out of a nightmare, and at first I thought that it was the beginning of another. Before falling asleep, I had heard dull noises coming from the direction of the laboratory, part of which lay directly over my cabin. It sounded like heavy objects and machinery being shifted. When I realized that I was not dreaming, I decided that the scream also came from above, but could not understand how it managed to penetrate the sound-proof ceiling. The terrible sounds went on for almost half an hour, until my nerves jangled and I was pouring with sweat. I was about to go up and investigate when the screaming stopped, to be replaced by more muffled sounds as of objects being dragged across the floor.

Rheya and I were sitting in the kitchen two days later when Snow came in. He was dressed as people dress on Earth after their day's work, and looked like a different person, taller and older. He did not look at us, or pull up a chair, but stood at the table, opened a can of meat and began cramming it down between mouthfuls of bread. His jacket sleeve brushed against the greasy top of the can.

'Look out, Snow, your sleeve!'

'What?' he grunted, then went on stuffing himself with food as if he had not eaten for days. He poured out a glass of wine, drank it at a gulp, sighed, and wiped his lips. Then he looked at me with bloodshot eyes, and mumbled:

'So you've stopped shaving? Ah . . .'

Rheya cleared the table. Snow swayed on his heels, then pulled a face and sucked his teeth noisily, deliberately exaggerating the action. He stared at me insistently:

'So you've decided not to shave?' I made no reply. 'Believe me,' he went on, 'you're making a mistake. That was how it started with him to . . .'

'Go and lie down.'

'What? Just when I feel like talking? Listen, Kelvin, perhaps it wishes well . . . perhaps it wants to please us but doesn't quite know how to set about the job. It spies out desires in our brains, and only two per cent of mental processes are conscious. That means it knows us better than we know ourselves. We've got to reach an understanding with it. Are you listening? Don't you want to? Why?' – he was sobbing by now – 'why don't you shave?'

'Shut up! . . . You're drunk.'

'Me, drunk? And what if I am? Just because I drift about from one end of space to another and poke my nose into the cosmos, does that mean I'm not allowed to get drunk? Why not? You believe in the Mission of Mankind, don't you, Kelvin? Gibarian told me about you before he started letting his beard grow . . . It was a very good description. Just don't go to the lab, if you don't want to lose your faith. It belongs to Sartorius – Faust in reverse . . . he's looking for a cure for immortality! He is the last Knight of the Holy Contact, the man we need. His latest discovery is pretty good too . . . prolonged dying. Not bad, eh? *Agonia perpetua* . . . of the straw . . . the straw hats . . . and still you don't drink, Kelvin?'

He raised his swollen eyelids and looked at Rheya, who was standing quite still with her back to the wall. Then he began chanting:

'O fair Aphrodite, child of Ocean, your divine hand . . .' He choked with laughter. 'It fits, eh, Kel . . .vin . . .'

He broke off in a fit of coughing.

'Shut up! Shut up and get out!' I grated through clenched teeth.

'You're chucking me out? You too? You don't shave and you chuck me out? What about my warnings, and my advice? Interstellar colleagues ought to help each other! Listen, Kelvin, let's go down and open the traps and call out. It might hear us. But what's its name? We have named all the stars and all the planets, even though they might already have had names of their own. What a nerve! Come on, let's go down. We'll shout it such a description of the trick it's played us that it will be touched. It will make us silver symmetriads, pray to us in calculus, send us its bloodstained angels. It will share our troubles and terrors, and beg us to help it die. It is already begging us, imploring us. It implores us to help it die with every one of its creations. You're not amused . . . but you know I'm just a joker. If man had more of a sense of humour, things might have turned out differently. Do you know what he wants to do? He wants to punish this ocean, hear it screaming out of all its mountains at once. If you think he'll never have the nerve to submit his plan to that bunch of doddering ancients who sent us here to redeem sins we haven't committed, you're right – he is afraid. But he is only afraid of the little hat. He won't let anybody see the little hat, he won't dare, not Faust . . .'

I said nothing. Snow's swaying increased. Tears were streaming down his cheeks and on to his clothes. He went on:

'Who is responsible? Who is responsible for this situation? Gibarian? Giese? Einstein? Plato? All criminals . . . Just you think, in a rocket a man takes the risk of bursting like a balloon, or freezing, or roasting, or sweating all his blood out in a single gush, before he can even cry out, and all that remains is bits of bone floating inside armoured hulls, in accordance with the laws of Newton as corrected by Einstein, those two milestones in our progress. Down the road we go, all in good faith, and see where it gets us. Think about our success, Kelvin; think about our cabins, the unbreakable plates, the immortal sinks, legions of faithful wardrobes, devoted cupboards . . . I wouldn't be talking this way if I weren't drunk, but sooner or later somebody was bound to say it, weren't they? You sit there like a baby in a slaughterhouse, and you let your beard grow . . . Who's to blame? Find out for yourself.'

He turned slowly and went out, putting an arm out against the doorpost to steady himself. Then his footsteps died away along the corridor.

I tried not to look at Rheya, but my eyes were drawn to hers in spite of myself. I wanted to get up, take her in my arms and stroke her hair. I did not move.

Victory

Another three weeks. The shutters rose and fell on time. I was still a prisoner in my nightmares, and every morning the play began again. But was it a play? I put on a feigned composure, and Rheya played the same game. The deception was mutual and deliberate, and our agreement only contributed to our ultimate evasion. We talked about the future, and our life on Earth on the outskirts of some great city. We would spend the rest of our lives among green trees and under a blue sky, and never leave Earth again. Together we planned the layout of our house and garden and argued over details like the location of a hedge or a bench.

I do not believe that I was sincere for a single instant. Our plans were impossible, and I knew it, or even if Rheya could leave the Station and survive the voyage, how could I have got through the immigration checks with my clandestine passenger? Earth admits only human beings, and even then only when they carry the necessary papers. Rheya would be detained for an identity check at the first barrier, we would be separated, and she would give herself away at once. The Station was the one place where we could live together. Rheya must have known that, or found it out.

One night I heard Rheya get out of bed silently. I wanted to stop her; in the darkness and silence we occasionally managed to throw off our despair for a while by making each other forget. Rheya did not notice that I had woken up. When I stretched my hand out, she was already out of bed, and walking barefoot towards the door. Without daring to raise my voice, I whispered her name, but she was outside, and a narrow shaft of light shone through the doorway from the corridor.

There was a sound of whispering. Rheya was talking to somebody . . . but who? Panic overtook me when I tried to stand up, and my legs would not move. I listened, but heard nothing. The blood hammered through my temples. I started counting, and was approaching a thousand when there was a movement in the doorway and Rheya returned. She stood there for a second without moving, and I made myself breathe evenly.

'Kris?' she whispered.

I did not answer.

She slid quickly into bed and lay down, taking care not to disturb me. Questions buzzed in my mind, but I would not let myself be the first to speak, and made no move. The silent questioning went on for an hour, maybe more. Then I fell asleep.

The morning was like any other. I watched Rheya furtively, but could not see any change in her behaviour. After breakfast, we sat at the big panoramic window. The Station was hovering among purple clouds. Rheya was reading, and as I stared out I suddenly noticed that by holding my head at a certain angle I could see us both reflected in the window. I took my hand off the rail. Rheya had no idea that I was watching her. She glanced at me, obviously decided from my posture that I was looking at the ocean, then bent to kiss the place where my hand had rested. In a moment she was reading her book again.

'Rheya,' I asked gently, 'where did you go last night?'

'Last night?'

'Yes.'

'You . . . you must have been dreaming, Kris. I didn't go anywhere.'

'You didn't leave the cabin?'

'No. It must have been a dream.'

'Perhaps . . . yes, perhaps I dreamt it.'

The same evening, I started talking about our return to Earth again, but Rheya stopped me:

'Don't talk to me about the journey again, Kris. I don't want to hear any more about it, you know very well . . .'

'What?'

'No, nothing.'

After we went to bed, she said that she was thirsty:

'There's a glass of fruit-juice on the table over there. Could you give it to me?' She drank half of it then handed it to me.

'I'm not thirsty.'

'Drink to my health then.' She smiled.

It tasted slightly bitter, but my mind was on other things. She switched the light off.

'Rheya . . . If you won't talk about the voyage, let's talk about something else.'

'If I did not exist, would you marry?'

'No.'

'Never?'

'Never.'

'Why not?'

'I don't know. I was by myself for ten years and I didn't marry again. Let's not talk about that . . .' My head was spinning as if I had been drinking too much.

'No, let's talk about it. What if I begged you to?'

'To marry again? Don't be silly, Rheya. I don't need anybody except you.'

I felt her breath on my face and her arms holding me:

'Say it another way.'

'I love you.'

Her head fell to my shoulder, and I felt tears.

'Rheya, what's the matter?'

'Nothing . . . nothing . . . nothing . . .' Her voice echoed into silence, and my eyes closed.

The red dawn woke me with a splitting head and a neck so stiff that I felt as if the bones were welded together. My tongue was swollen, and my mouth felt foul. Then I reached out for Rheya, and my hand touched a cold sheet.

I sat up with a start.

I was alone – alone in bed and in the cabin. The concave window reflected a row of red suns. I dragged myself out of bed and staggered over to the bathroom, reeling like a drunkard and propping myself up on the furniture. It was empty. So was the workshop.

'Rheya!'

Calling, running up and down the corridor.

'Rheya!' I screamed, one last time, then my voice gave out. I already knew the truth . . .

I do not remember the exact sequence of events after that, as I stumbled half naked through all the length and breadth of the Station. It seems to me that I even went into the refrigeration section, searched through the storage-rooms, hammered with my fists on bolted doors then came back again to throw myself against doors which had already resisted me. I half fell down flights of steps, picked myself up and hurried onwards. When I reached the double armoured doors which opened on to the ocean I was still calling, still hoping that it was a dream. Somebody was standing by me. Hands took hold of me and pulled me away.

I came to my senses again lying on a metal table in the little workshop and gasping for breath. My throat and nostrils were burning with some alcoholic vapour, my shirt was soaked in water, and my hair plastered over my skull.

Snow was busy at a medicine-cupboard, shifting instruments and glass vessels which clattered with an unbearable din. Then his face appeared, looking gravely down into my eyes.

'Where is she?'

'She is not here.'

'But . . . Rheya . . .'

He bent over me, brought his face closer, and spoke very slowly and clearly:

'Rheya is dead.'

'She will come back,' I whispered.

Instead of dreading her return, I wanted it. I did not

attempt to remind myself why I had once tried to drive her away, and why I had been so afraid of her return.

'Drink this.'

Snow held out a glass, and I threw it in his face. He staggered back, rubbing his eyes, and by the time he opened them again I was on my feet and standing over him. How small he was . . .

'It was you.'

'What do you mean?'

'Come on, Snow, you know what I mean. It was you who met her the other night. You told her to give me a sleeping pill . . . What has happened to her? Tell me!'

He felt in his shirt-pocket and took out an envelope. I snatched it out of his hand. It was sealed, and there was no inscription. Inside was a sheet of paper folded twice, and I recognized the sprawling, rather childish handwriting:

My darling, I was the one who asked him. He is a good man. I am sorry I had to lie to you. I beg you to give me this one wish – hear him out, and do nothing to harm yourself. You have been marvellous.

There was one more word, which she had crossed out, but I could see that she had signed 'Rheya'.

My mind was now absolutely clear. Even if I had wanted to scream hysterically, my voice had gone, and I did not even have the strength to groan.

'How . . .?'

'Later, Kelvin. You've got to calm down.'

'I'm calm now. Tell me how.'

'Disintegration.'

'But . . . what did you use?'

'The Roche apparatus was unsuitable. Sartorius built something else, a new destabilizer. A miniature instrument, with a range of a few yards.'

'And she . . .'

'She disappeared. A pop, and a puff of air. That's all.'

'A short-range instrument . . .'

'Yes, we didn't have the resources for anything bigger.'

The walls loomed over me, and I shut my eyes.

'She will come back.'

'No.'

'What do you know about it?'

'You remember the wings of foam? Since that day, they do not come back.'

'You killed her,' I whispered.

'Yes . . . In my place, what else would you have done?'

I turned away from him and began pacing up and down the room. Nine steps to the corner. About turn. Nine more rapid steps, and I was facing Snow again.

'Listen, we'll write a report. We'll ask for an immediate link with the Council. It's feasible, and they'll accept – they must. The planet will no longer be subject to the four-power convention. We'll be authorized to use any means at our disposal. We can send for anti-matter generators. Nothing can stand up against them, nothing . . .' I was shouting now, and blinded with tears.

'You want to destroy it? Why?'

'Get out, leave me alone!'

'No, I won't get out.'

'Snow!' I glared at him, and he shook his head. 'What do you want? What am I supposed to do?'

He walked back to the table.

'Fine, we'll draw up a report.'

I started pacing again.

'Sit down!'

'I'll do what I like!'

'There are two distinct questions. One, the facts. Two, our recommendations.'

'Do we have to talk about it now?'

'Yes, now.'

'I won't listen, you hear? I'm not interested in your distinctions.'

200

'We sent our last message about two months ago, before Gibarian's death. We'll have to establish exactly how the "visitor" phenomena function . . .'

I grabbed his arm:

'Will you shut up!'

'Hit me if you like, but I will not shut up.'

'Oh, talk away, if it gives you pleasure . . .' I let him go.

'Good, listen. Sartorius will want to conceal certain facts. I'm almost certain of it.'

'And what about you? Won't you conceal anything?'

'No. Not now. This business goes further than individual responsibilities. You know that as well as I do. "It" has given a demonstration of considered activity. It is capable of carrying out organic synthesis on the most complex level, a synthesis we ourselves have never managed to achieve. It knows the structure, micro-structure and metabolism of our bodies . . .'

'All right . . . But why stop there? It has performed a series of . . . experiments on us. Psychic vivisection. It has used knowledge which it stole from our minds without our consent.'

'Those are not facts, Kelvin. They are not even propositions. They are theories. You could say that it has taken account of desires locked into secret recesses of our brains. Perhaps it was sending us . . . presents.'

'Presents! My God!' I shook with a fit of uncontrollable laughter.

'Take it easy!' Snow took hold of my hand, and I tightened my grip until I heard bones cracking. He went on looking at me without any change of expression. I let go, and walked over to a corner of the workshop:

'I'll try to get hold of myself.'

'Yes, of course. I understand. What do we ask them?'

'I leave it to you . . . I can't think straight right now. Did she say anything – before?'

'No, nothing. If you want my opinion, from now on we stand a chance.'

'A chance? What chance?' I stared at him, and light suddenly dawned. 'Contact? Still Contact? Haven't you had enough of this madhouse? What more do you need? No, it's out of the question. Count me out!'

'Why not,' he asked quietly. 'You yourself instinctively treat it like a human being, now more than ever. You hate it.'

'And you don't?'

'No, Kelvin. It is blind . . .' I thought that I might not have heard him correctly. '. . . or rather it "sees" in a different way from ourselves. We do not exist for it in the same sense that we exist for each other. We recognize one another by the appearance of the face and the body. That appearance is a transparent window to the ocean. It introduces itself directly into the brain.'

'Right, what if it does? What are you driving at? It succeeded in re-creating a human being who exists only in my memory, and so accurately that her eyes, her gestures, her voice . . .'

'Don't stop. Talk.'

'I'm talking . . . Her voice . . . because it is able to read us like a book. You see what I mean?'

'Yes, that it could make itself understood.'

'Doesn't that follow?'

'No, not necessarily. Perhaps it used a formula which is not expressed in verbal terms. It may be taken from a recording imprinted on our minds, but a man's memory is stored in terms of nucleic acids etching asynchronous large-moleculed crystals. "It" removed the deepest, most isolated imprint, the most "assimilated" structure, without necessarily knowing what it meant to us. Suppose, I'm capable of reproducing the architecture of a symmetriad, and I know its composition and have the requisite technology . . . I create a symmetriad and I drop it into the ocean. But I don't know why I'm doing so, I don't know its function, and I don't know what the symmetriad means to the ocean . . .'

'Yes. You may be right. In that case it wished us no harm, and it was not trying to destroy us. Yes, it's possible . . . and with no intention . . .'

My mouth began to tremble.

'Kelvin!'

'All right, don't get worried. You are kind, the ocean is kind. Everybody is kind. But why? Explain that. Why has it done this? What did you say . . . to her?'

'The truth.'

'I asked you what you said.'

'You know very well. Come back to my cabin and we'll write out the report. Come on.'

'Wait. What exactly do you want? You can't be intending to remain in the Station.'

'Yes, I want to stay.'

The Old Mimoid

I sat by the panoramic window, looking at the ocean. There was nothing to do now that the report, which had taken five days to compile, was only a pattern of waves in space. It would be months before a similar pattern would leave Earth to create its own line of disturbance in the gravitational field of the galaxy towards the twin suns of Solaris.

Under the red sun, the ocean was darker than ever, and the horizon was obscured by a reddish mist. The weather was unusually close, and seemed to be building up towards one of the terrible hurricanes which broke out two or three times a year on the surface of the planet, whose sole inhabitant, it is reasonable to suppose, controlled the climate and willed its storms.

There were several months to go before I could leave. From my vantage point in the observatory I would watch the birth of the days – a disc of pale gold or faded purple. Now and then I would come upon the light of dawn playing among the fluid forms of some edifice risen from the ocean, watch the sun reflected on the silver sphere of a symmetriad, follow the oscillations of the graceful agiluses that curve in the wind, and linger to examine old powdery mimoids.

And eventually, the screens of all the videophones would start to blink and all the communications equipment would spring to life again, revived by an impulse originating billions of miles away and announcing the arrival of a metal colossus. The *Ulysses*, or it might be the *Prometheus*, would land on the Station to the piercing whine of its gravitors, and I would go out on to the flat roof to watch the squads of white, heavy-duty robots which proceed in all innocence with their tasks, not hesitating to destroy themselves or to destroy the unforeseen obstacle, in strict obedience to the orders etched into the crystals of their memory. Then the ship would rise noiselessly, faster than sound, leaving a sonic boom far behind over the ocean, and every passenger's face would light up at the thought of going home.

What did that word mean to me? Earth? I thought of the great bustling cities where I would wander and lose myself, and I thought of them as I had thought of the ocean on the second or third night, when I had wanted to throw myself upon the dark waves. I shall immerse myself among men. I shall be silent and attentive, an appreciative companion. There will be many acquaintances, friends, women – and perhaps even a wife. For a while, I shall have to make a conscious effort to smile, nod, stand and perform the thousands of little gestures which constitute life on Earth, and then those gestures will become reflexes again. I shall find new interests and occupations; and I shall not give myself completely to them, as I shall never again give myself completely to anything or anybody. Perhaps at night I shall stare up at the dark nebula that cuts off the light of the twin suns, and remember everything, even what I am thinking now. With a condescending, slightly rueful smile I shall remember my follies and my hopes. And this future Kelvin will be no less worthy a man than the Kelvin of the past, who was prepared for anything in the name of an ambitious enterprise called Contact. Nor will any man have the right to judge me.

Snow came into the cabin, glanced around, then looked at me again. I went over to the table:

'You wanted me?'

'Haven't you got anything to do? I could give you some work . . . calculations. Not a particularly urgent job . . .'

'Thanks,' I smiled, 'you needn't have bothered.'

'Are you sure?'

'Yes, I was thinking a few things over, and . . .'

'I wish you'd think a little less.'

'But you don't know what I was thinking about! Tell me something. Do you believe in God?'

Snow darted an apprehensive glance in my direction:

'What? Who still believes nowadays . . .'

'It isn't that simple. I don't mean the traditional God of Earth religion. I'm no expert in the history of religions and perhaps this is nothing new – do you happen to know if there was ever a belief in an . . . imperfect god?'

'What do you mean by imperfect?' Snow frowned. 'In a way all the gods of the old religions were imperfect, considering that their attributes were amplified human ones. The God of the Old Testament, for instance, required humble submission and sacrifices, and was jealous of other gods. The Greek gods had fits of sulks and family quarrels, and they were just as imperfect as mortals . . .'

'No,' I interrupted. 'I'm not thinking of a god whose imperfection arises out of the candour of his human creators, but one whose imperfection represents his essential characteristic: a god limited in his omniscience and power, fallible, incapable of foreseeing the consequences of his acts, and creating things that lead to horror. He is a . . . sick god, whose ambitions exceed his powers and who does not realize it at first. A god who has created clocks, but not the time they measure. He has created systems or mechanisms that served specific ends but have now overstepped and betrayed them. And he has created eternity, which was to have measured his power, and which measures his unending defeat.'

Snow hesitated, but his attitude no longer showed any of the wary reserve of recent weeks:

'There was Manicheanism . . .'

'Nothing at all to do with the principle of Good and Evil,' I broke in immediately. 'This god has no existence outside of matter. He would like to free himself from matter, but he cannot . . .'

Snow pondered for a while:

'I don't know of any religion that answers your description. That kind of religion has never been . . . necessary. If I understand you, and I'm afraid I do, what you have in mind is an evolving god, who develops in the course of time, grows, and keeps increasing in power while remaining aware of his powerlessness. For your god, the divine condition is a situation without a goal. And understanding that, he despairs. But isn't this despairing god of yours mankind, Kelvin? It is man you are talking about, and that is a fallacy, not just philosophically but also mystically speaking.'

I kept on:

'No, it's nothing to do with man. Man may correspond to my provisional definition from some points of view, but that is because the definition has a lot of gaps. Man does not create gods, in spite of appearances. The times, the age, impose them on him. Man can serve his age or rebel against it, but the target of his cooperation or rebellion comes to him from outside. If there was only a single human being in existence, he would apparently be able to attempt the experiment of creating his own goals in complete freedom – apparently, because a man not brought up among other human beings cannot become a man. And the being – the being I have in mind – cannot exist in the plural, you see?'

'Oh, then in that case . . . ' He pointed out of the window.

'No, not the ocean either. Somewhere in its development it has probably come close to the divine state, but it turned back into itself too soon. It is more like an anchorite, a hermit of the cosmos, not a god. It repeats itself, Snow, and the being I'm thinking of would never do that. Perhaps he has already been born somewhere, in some corner of the galaxy, and soon he will have some childish enthusiasm that will set him putting out one star and lighting another. We will notice him after a while . . . '

'We already have,' Snow said sarcastically. 'Novas and supernovas. According to you they are the candles on his altar.'

'If you're going to take what I say literally . . .'

'And perhaps Solaris is the cradle of your divine child,' Snow went on, with a widening grin that increased the number of lines round his eyes. 'Solaris could be the first phase of the despairing god. Perhaps its intelligence will grow enormously. All the contents of our Solarist libraries could be just a record of his teething troubles . . .'

'. . . and we will have been the baby's toys for a while. It is possible. And do you know what you have just done? You've produced a completely new hypothesis about Solaris – congratulations! Everything suddenly falls into place: the failure to achieve Contact, the absence of responses, various . . . let's say various peculiarities in its behaviour towards ourselves. Everything is explicable in terms of the behaviour of a small child.'

'I renounce paternity of the theory,' Snow grunted, standing at the window.

For a long instant, we stood staring out at the dark waves. A long pale patch was coming into view to the east, in the mist obscuring the horizon.

Without taking his eyes off the shimmering waste, Snow asked abruptly:

'What gave you this idea of an imperfect god?'

'I don't know. It seems quite feasible to me. That is the only god I could imagine believing in, a god whose passion is not a redemption, who saves nothing, fulfils no purpose – a god who simply is.'

'A mimoid,' Snow breathed.

'What's that? Oh yes, I'd noticed it. A very old mimoid.'

We both looked towards the misty horizon.

'I'm going outside,' I said abruptly. 'I've never yet been off the Station, and this is a good opportunity. I'll be back in half an hour.'

Snow raised his eyebrows:

'What? You're going out? Where are you going?'

I pointed towards the flesh-coloured patch half hidden by the mist:

'Over there. What is there to stop me? I'll take a small helicopter. When I get back to Earth I don't want to have to confess that I'm a Solarist who has never set foot on Solaris!'

I opened a locker and started rummaging through the atmosphere suits, while Snow looked on silently. Finally he said:

'I don't like it.'

I had selected a suit. Now I turned towards him:

'What?' I had not felt so excited for a long time. 'What are you worrying about? Out with it! You're afraid that I . . . I promise you I have no intention . . . it never entered my mind, honestly.'

'I'll go with you.'

'Thanks, but I'd rather go alone.' I pulled on the suit. 'Do you realize this will be my first flight over the ocean?'

Snow muttered something, but I could not make out what. I was in a hurry to get the rest of the gear together.

He accompanied me to the hangar-deck, and helped me drag the flitter out on to the elevator disc. As I was checking my suit, he asked me abruptly:

'Can I rely on your word?'

'Still fretting? Yes, you can. Where are the oxygen-tanks?'

We exchanged no further words. I slid the transparent canopy shut, gave him the signal, and he set the lift going. I emerged on to the Station roof; the motor burst into life; the three blades turned and the machine rose – strangely light – into the air. Soon the Station had fallen far behind.

Alone over the ocean, I saw it with a different eye. I was flying quite low, at about a hundred feet, and for the first time I felt a sensation often described by the explorers but which I had never noticed from the height of the Station: the alternating motion of the gleaming waves was not at all like the undulation of the sea or the billowing of clouds. It was like the crawling skin of an animal – the incessant, slow-motion contractions of muscular flesh secreting a crimson foam.

When I started to bank towards the drifting mimoid, the sun shone into my eyes and blood-red flashes struck the curved canopy. The dark ocean, flickering with sombre flames, was tinged with blue.

The flitter came around too wide, and I was carried a long way downwind from the mimoid, a long irregular silhouette looming out of the ocean. Emerging from the mist, the mimoid was no longer pink, but a yellowish grey. I lost sight of it momentarily, and glimpsed the Station, which seemed to be sitting on the horizon, and whose outline was reminiscent of an ancient zeppelin. I changed course, and the sheer mass of the mimoid grew in my line of vision – a baroque sculpture. I was afraid of crashing into the bulbous swellings, and pulled the flitter up so brutally that it lost speed and started to lurch; but my caution was unnecessary, for the rounded peaks of those fantastic towers were subsiding.

I flew past the island; and slowly, yard by yard, I descended to the level of the eroded peaks. The mimoid was not large. It measured about three-quarters of a mile from end to end, and was a few hundred yards wide. In some places, it was close to splitting apart. This mimoid was obviously a fragment of a far larger formation. On the scale of Solaris it was only a tiny splinter, weeks or perhaps months old.

Among the mottled crags overhanging the ocean, I found a kind of beach, a sloping, fairly even surface a few yards square, and steered towards it. The rotors almost hit a cliff that reared up suddenly in my path, but I landed safely, cut the motor and slid back the canopy. Standing on the fuselage I made sure that there was no chance of the flitter sliding into the ocean. Waves were licking at the jagged bank about fifteen paces away, but the machine rested solidly on its legs, and I jumped to the 'ground'.

The cliff I had almost hit was a huge bony membrane pierced with holes, and full of knotty swellings. A crack several yards wide split this wall diagonally and enabled me to examine the interior of the island, already glimpsed through the apertures in the membrane. I edged warily on to the nearest ledge, but my boots showed no tendency to slide and the suit did not impede my movements, and I went on climbing until I had reached a height of about four storeys above the ocean, and could see a broad stretch of petrified landscape stretching back until it was lost from sight in the depths of the mimoid.

It was like looking at the ruins of an ancient town, a Moroccan city tens of centuries old, convulsed by an earthquake or some other disaster. I made out a tangled web of winding sidestreets choked with debris, and alleyways which fell abruptly towards the oily foam that floated close to the shore. In the middle distance, great battlements stood intact, sustained by ossified buttresses. There were dark openings in the swollen, sunken walls – traces of windows or loop-holes. The whole of this floating town canted to one side or another like a foundering ship, pitched and turned slowly, and the sun cast continually moving shadows, which crept among the ruined alleys. Now and again a polished surface caught and reflected the light. I took the risk of climbing higher, then stopped; rivulets of fine sand were beginning to trickle down the rocks above my head, cascading into ravines and alleyways and rebounding in swirling clouds of dust. The mimoid is not made of stone, and to dispel the illusion one only has to pick up a piece of it: it is lighter than pumice, and composed of small, very porous cells.

Now I was high enough to feel the swaying of the mimoid. It was moving forward, propelled by the dark muscles of the ocean towards an unknown destination, but its inclination varied. It rolled from side to side, and the languid oscillation was accompanied by the gentle rustling sound of the yellow and grey foam which streamed off the emerging shore. The mimoid had acquired its swinging motion long before, probably at its birth, and even while it grew and broke up it had retained its initial pattern.

Only now did I realize that I was not in the least concerned with the mimoid, and that I had flown here not to explore the formation but to acquaint myself with the ocean.

With the flitter a few paces behind me, I sat on the rough, fissured beach. A heavy black wave broke over the edge of the bank and spread out, not black, but a dirty green. The ebbing wave left viscous streamlets behind, which flowed back quivering towards the ocean. I went closer, and when the next wave came I held out my hand.

What followed was a faithful reproduction of a phenomenon which had been analysed a century before: the wave hesitated, recoiled, then enveloped my hand without touching it, so that a thin covering of 'air' separated my glove inside a cavity which had been fluid a moment previously, and now had a fleshy consistency. I raised my hand slowly, and the wave, or rather an outcrop of the wave, rose at the same time, enfolding my hand in a translucent cyst with greenish reflections. I stood up, so as to raise my hand still higher, and the gelatinous substance stretched like a rope, but did not break. The main body of the wave remained motionless on the shore, surrounding my feet without touching them, like some strange beast patiently waiting for the experiment to finish. A flower had grown out of the ocean, and its calyx was moulded to my fingers. I stepped back. The stem trembled, stirred uncertainly and fell back into the wave, which gathered it and receded.

I repeated the game several times, until – as the first experimenter had observed – a wave arrived which avoided me indifferently, as if bored with a too familiar sensation. I knew that to revive the 'curiosity' of the ocean I would have to wait several hours. Disturbed by the phenomenon I had stimulated, I sat down again. Although I had read numerous accounts of it, none of them had prepared me for the experience as I had lived it, and I felt somehow changed.

In all their movements, taken together or singly, each of these branches reaching out of the ocean seemed to display a kind of cautious but not feral alertness, a curiosity avid for quick apprehension of a new, unexpected form, and regretful at having to retreat, unable to exceed the limits set by a mysterious law. The contrast was inexpressible between that lively curiosity and the shimmering immensity of the ocean that stretched away out of sight . . . I had never felt its gigantic presence so strongly, or its powerful changeless silence, or the secret forces that gave the waves their regular rise and fall. I sat unseeing, and sank into a universe of inertia, glided down an irresistible slope and identified myself with the dumb, fluid colossus; it was as if I had forgiven it everything, without the slightest effort of word or thought.

During that last week, I had been behaving so normally that Snow had stopped keeping a watchful eye on me. On the surface, I was calm: in secret, without really admitting it, I was waiting for something. Her return? How could I have been waiting for that? We all know that we are material creatures, subject to the laws of physiology and physics, and not even the power of all our feelings combined can defeat those laws. All we can do is detest them. The age-old faith of lovers and poets in the power of love, stronger than death, that *finis vitae sed non amoris*, is a lie, useless and not even funny. So must one be resigned to being a clock that measures the passage of time, now out of order, now repaired, and whose mechanism generates despair and love as soon as its maker sets it going? Are we to grow used to the idea that every man relives ancient torments, which are all the more profound because they grow comic with repetition? That human existence should repeat itself, well and good, but that it should repeat itself like a hackneyed tune, or a record a drunkard keeps playing as he feeds coins into the jukebox . . .

That liquid giant had been the death of hundreds of men. The entire human race had tried in vain to establish even the most tenuous link with it, and it bore my weight without

213

noticing me any more than it would notice a speck of dust. I did not believe that it could respond to the tragedy of two human beings. Yet its activities did have a purpose . . . True, I was not absolutely certain, but leaving would mean giving up a chance, perhaps an infinitesimal one, perhaps only imaginary . . . Must I go on living here then, among the objects we both had touched, in the air she had breathed? In the name of what? In the hope of her return? I hoped for nothing. And yet I lived in expectation. Since she had gone, that was all that remained. I did not know what achievements, what mockery, even what tortures still awaited me. I knew nothing, and I persisted in the faith that the time of cruel miracles was not past.